The Tab

A History
of
Gillingham Baptist Church

By

Stephen Greasley

British Library Cataloguing in Publication Data.
A catalogue record for this book is available
from the British Library.

ISBN 978 086071 689 1

A Commissioned Publication of

MOORLEYS
Print & Publishing
tel: 0115 932 0643 web: www.moorleys.co.uk

CONTENTS

ACKNOWLEDGEMENTS

I am greatly indebted to a number of people who have made the compilation of this volume possible. Mr J.W. Winfield died in 1968 but I like to think of his fingerprints all over this book. It was his careful and methodical preservation of records which made it possible to unearth the story of those early and middle years of the church's history. His own volume, "These Eighty Years," produced in 1959 provided a useful starting point. But it was his collection and collation of letters, copies of the 'Tabernacle Tidings', and copies of the Kent and Sussex Association handbooks, that made researching this project relatively easy. Both Mr Winfield and earlier Church Secretaries have done posterity a favour by the careful collection of newspaper articles relating to events in the life of the "Tabernacle (Tab.)". Many of these have been attached to Church Meeting Minute books or Church Membership Rolls, and have proved an invaluable additional resource. Ever the historian, Mr Winfield prepared the ground for those who would come after him.

I would like to place on record my gratitude to Geoffrey and Beryl Breed whose friendship and encouragement throughout my time in Gillingham helped to rekindle my own interest in local church history. Walking into Geoffrey's study back in 2011 was akin to the small schoolboy being let loose in the chocolate factory. I couldn't believe the historical goodies that lay before me! As former archivist for the Kent Baptist Association and inveterate collector of Baptist historical literature Geoffrey has been quite inspirational. The fact that he and Beryl were key workers at the Tab. for over twenty years, and still retain a keen memory of things from the 1960s and 1970s, has helped to refine the text for that period. I am also indebted to them for proof reading the early drafts of this book and correcting both some glaring errors and my own clumsy grammar!

I would also like to express my appreciation to two of my former colleagues, Rev Chris Voke and Rev David John, for their own recollections of this period and passing helpful comments on my early drafts. Reg and Christine Hughes very kindly improved the text of chapters 8, 9 and 10 which covered the period in which they exercised key leadership roles in the church. Similarly, I am indebted to Hilary Cox and Lyn Newlan whose years of service at Gillingham Baptist Church made them perfectly suited to proof reading sections of the book as well as bringing their own understanding to what was happening at the time. Sue Wilkins also has been a real treasure in kindly going over the entire manuscript with a fine tooth comb and has immeasurably improved the text as a result.

So many people have obliged me by providing photographs of key events and personnel of the last 40 years. But my particular thanks must go to David Howlett whose patience in scanning endless musty photographs from the church archives made my job so much easier and relieved me of what was likely to become a very daunting burden. My own son, David Greasley, also came to the rescue in arranging the photographic sections of the book which his father seemed incapable of sorting out!

The staff at the Angus Library in Oxford, the Local Studies Library in Strood, and the Spurgeon's College archive deserve my special thanks for their kindliness and hospitality. Ann Hardy also helpfully provided me with some material pertaining to Camden Road Baptist Church for which I am most grateful.

I am also indebted to Moorleys Print and Publishing Ltd of Ilkeston for agreeing to produce this book. While it may seem strange to produce a book on Kent history over in Derbyshire, it was my past connections with them that persuaded me that they were the right people to handle this publication. Their careful attention to detail, their professionalism, and their accommodating manner have made this whole process both encouraging and enjoyable. The finished product bears testimony to the fact that they were indeed the right people to handle this book.

Finally, I need to apologise for a number of inconsistencies in the text. There are times when I have called someone 'Rev' and other times when I have simply referred to them as 'Mr'. Sometimes I may have called someone 'minister' and other times I may refer to them as 'pastor'. Sometimes I may have referred to a person with their initials, such as C.J. Pike, other times I may have given them their full name, e.g. Jack Pike or simply Mr Pike. These inconsistencies may in part be due to my own lack of rigour. But equally they may arise from the different ways names are recorded in the minutes. As a general rule of thumb I have tried to lift the names as they are written down in the various books. And because different hands have produced these written records then different ways of recording names have also occurred. In going over the text I have tried to iron out some of these inconsistencies, but this has not always been possible. It also needs to be borne in mind that in earlier records there was a far more formal way of recording names than in the modern era.

I do hope that you will enjoy reading this volume. I think the record of the past is well worth re-telling for the present generation. There are lessons to be learned. Moreover, the heroes of one generation soon become forgotten. This book is a small attempt to recall their names and their contribution for posterity.

While it is good to look back it is also vital that we look to the future as well. The story of Gillingham Baptist Church is still being written. Even as this book goes to print major decisions are being made about the future of these old buildings and what the place will look like in the coming years. To that end, all the proceeds of this book will go towards the Gillingham Baptist Church 'Fund for the Future', and will in some small measure contribute to the on-going story of this place and its people. The work of God is not simply to be traced in the annals of church history, but in the unfolding story fleshed out by a new generation.

INTRODUCTION

The story of Gillingham Baptist Church is the story of so many churches at the close of the Victorian era. It begins with **Vision.** A small group of Baptist Christians meeting over in Chatham but living in Gillingham decided that they needed a worshipping centre in their own town. The vision gave birth to a passion, and a growing determination to bring about what they had set their hearts upon. It is a story that was replicated time and again at the end of the nineteenth century. Along with vision we find a plentiful supply of **Faith.** This is the faith to believe that the impossible is possible; that seemingly insurmountable obstacles can be overcome; that from tiny acorns mighty oaks can and will grow. Such a small group of faith-full Christians would have been, at times, overwhelmed by the scale of the task before them. But they persevered. Their resources were meagre, but an indomitable spirit kept them going, and an unquenchable belief that God wanted this work to prosper and flourish.

To these attributes of Vision and Faith was added a third one: **Sacrifice.** So many of these church pioneers were tireless workers. They invested their time in the fledgling cause. They invested their energies in training up the young. They went without so that the work of God might prosper. They gave financially "as much as they were able, and even beyond their ability." (2 Corinthians 8:3). Any two of these factors would probably not have been enough to see through the construction of a magnificent place of worship and a growing and flourishing congregation. It required all three of these elements to be in place for the transformation to take place. Remarkably, in 140 years, nothing has changed. Vision, Faith and Sacrifice still remain the essential raw materials for the advancement of the Church of God.

It is true that circumstances were ripe for the planting of a church in Gillingham at the end of the nineteenth century. Between 1860 and 1910 Gillingham had the fifth fastest population growth in England. New housing was springing up everywhere in the town. New families were moving in. And in an age when church attendance was regarded as something important, and when there were few other social amenities to rival those provided by the church, these were very propitious times to start a new Non-Conformist cause in Gillingham. The phenomenal growth in church and Sunday School attendance in those early years bears this out.

There were, however, two other factors which made possible the remarkable birthing of this new church. One of these was the 'fortuitous' choice of Walter William Blocksidge as their first pastor. In church planting contexts getting the right pioneer minister is vital, and Gillingham managed to obtain the right man at just the right time. Blocksidge's own savvy, strong belief system, pastoral heart, and strong work ethic, along with his commitment to a settled pastorate were ideal qualities for this type of situation. Blocksidge clearly had a common touch that endeared him to people in a similar way to Tom Rogers two generations later. This helped to draw a loyal following of people. Both Blocksidge and Tom Rogers were inspirational figures. Their force of personality helped to make things happen, and the revivals that took place during their ministries cannot be separated from who they were as people.

But Blocksidge's appointment at Gillingham was itself no accident, and was in fact part of a larger master plan designed by that most influential and important Baptist of the nineteenth century, Charles Haddon Spurgeon. It is hard for us to imagine today, when religion has such a marginal hold on the public imagination, what a colossal influence C.H. Spurgeon had on British society. Spurgeon was a household name. He was a celebrity; a star, not of film or stage, but of the church. National and provincial newspapers carried stories about him. At times it seemed that every word he spoke and wrote was recorded and reported.

Spurgeon began a preaching ministry in London in 1854 while still not twenty years old. Such was the fame of his preaching that a whole new church building had to be constructed to accommodate the crowds he attracted week by week. The Metropolitan Tabernacle, completed in 1861 and seating six thousand people, was the base for his ministry for the next thirty years. But arguably Spurgeon's greatest achievements were not through his pulpit ministry but through his training several generations of students for the Baptist ministry. In 1857 the Pastors' College was officially started. In 1874 a magnificent building was opened to house the new College. From that point on the College sent hundreds of men, and later women, into the mission field in Great Britain and across the world.

Such was his influence, however, and such was his authority and reputation, that C.H. Spurgeon was able to direct his students in ways that would be unthinkable today. If a vacancy in a church pastorate came to his attention Spurgeon would take an active part in selecting one of his students for the post. Vacancies in overseas territories might emerge and Spurgeon would not hesitate in directing the person he felt best suited to fill that vacancy. So it was in 1878 that Spurgeon directed two of his junior students, Messrs Blackaby and Blocksidge, to New Brompton. It was Spurgeon again who was instrumental in settling Blackaby in his first church in Stow on the Wold; and Spurgeon again who strongly encouraged Blocksidge to accept the pastorate that had opened up in Gillingham. Blocksidge, in later autobiographical fragments, indicated his own severe hesitations about taking on the post, and was only persuaded by the 'gentle' encouragement of the great man himself.

But Spurgeon went one step further. By the 1870s he was a very wealthy man. His income from the Metropolitan Tabernacle, and the financial backing he received from various parts of the evangelical world, meant that he had at his disposal funds with which he could directly assist innumerable church building schemes. Spurgeon's name appears as a trustee of large numbers of Baptist churches formed in the latter quarter of the nineteenth century. He was Building Fund Treasurer of the New Brompton cause until his death in 1892. This was a role he exercised in many other places as well. Similarly, as with the New Brompton cause, Spurgeon's name was invariably chief among the benefactors of these various building funds. A millionaire by today's standards, Spurgeon used his money to bank roll a wave of building projects across a whole swathe of Southern England.

Spurgeon's generosity, however, was not restricted solely to the construction of Baptist church buildings. Perhaps most remarkable of all was the way that he personally took responsibility for the stipends of those of his students who were starting off in new and difficult areas. Spurgeon paid for the preaching expenses of Blackaby and Blocksidge until the small congregation could get on its feet financially. He made major financial contributions to Blocksidge's stipend when he started as pastor of the church. Indeed it was only Spurgeon's assurance that he would underwrite the initial stipend that allowed the fledgling church to invite Blocksidge in the first place.

Vision, Faith and Sacrifice were vital ingredients in the success of the Baptist cause in New Brompton. But it was the vision, faith and sacrifice of Charles Haddon Spurgeon that were just as significant. Frequently history reminds us that the life of one person can make a world of difference, and the legacy and impact of that one person can still be felt over one hundred years later. That was certainly the case back in 1878. It remains equally true today.

Stephen Greasley
Minister, Gillingham Baptist Church
August 2014

CHAPTER 1

BEGINNINGS

At the end of the nineteenth century Gillingham, or New Brompton as it was called, was a rapidly growing town. From a population of just over 4,000 people in 1801 it had more than doubled in size by 1851, and for the next sixty years saw a year on year growth so that by 1911 there were over 52,000 people living in the town[1]. From a quiet rural setting with extensive fields it was transformed into a major industrial town with row upon row of terraced houses. The expansion was in many ways generated by the growth of the Chatham dockyard which saw a rise in its workforce from less than 3,000 workers in 1840 to well over 9,000 by the outbreak of the First World War[2]. New schools were required to handle the burgeoning population. Schools on Richmond Road, Barnsole Road, Napier Road and Byron Road were all constructed at the end of the Victorian era or into the early Edwardian period[3]. Local Education Authority spending rose from just £650 in 1895 to £30,978 in 1906. That same period saw £145,608 spent on the building and maintenance of schools in the town[4].

It was not surprising, therefore, that into this new town there should be initiatives to plant and establish new churches. The Baptists were one of the first to take advantage of this promising new situation. On 27th December 1876 a Church Meeting at Enon Baptist Church, Chatham, recorded the following: "Since the last Church Meeting a place known as the Workmen's Hall, High St. New Brompton, has been hired for three months (hoping that the Lord will bless the undertaking) which will be opened for public worship on Lord's Day January 14th 1877 when Mr Banks of London has kindly consented to preach three sermons for the occasion." The cause clearly struggled because the minutes of the Enon Church Meeting on 28th March 1877 record a recommendation from the leadership that the hire of the Workmen's Hall be brought to a close after giving a month's notice. An amendment to this proposal was put by brother Foster, that the Hall should be hired for worship for another quarter. The amendment was passed by a majority of one.

William Foster had become a member of Enon Baptist Church in 1872. The Enon church records have him living at Lower Britton Street, New

1

Brompton. His wife, Mary, had become a member at Enon in 1864. They were part of a small group of members at Enon who lived over in New Brompton, and William was obviously anxious that the cause at the Workmen's Hall should continue. The Enon Church Meeting, however, did finally agree to end the hire of the Workmen's Hall by ten votes to five on 3rd October 1877. In consequence of this decision, on 27th March 1878 the Enon records relate that William Foster transferred his membership to Zion Baptist Church, Chatham. His wife continued on the Roll at Enon.

On May 11th 1878, however, a letter from five members of Enon to the Church Meeting formally requested "their dismission in order that they may be formed into a distinct church of the same faith and order at New Brompton." The five members were William and Eliza Drake, Martha Bridge, and Jabez and Celia Price. The letter says that after Enon had formally relinquished the hire of the Hall for public worship "one of the brethren here took the temporal responsibility of the cause upon himself."

Faced with the enthusiasm and commitment of this small group, the church at Enon agreed (May 22nd 1878) to formally release the five members to form a Strict Baptist Church in New Brompton. An account of this new cause is provided by William Drake in the Strict Baptist periodical, "the Earthen Vessel", in July 1878. The group worshipping in the Workmen's Hall formed themselves into a church on Sunday June 2nd. Jabez Price was deacon, William Drake was pastor, and the small group celebrated the Lord's Supper together. "This is the first Baptist Church in this town." Drake declared. In fact it can only have lasted for a matter of weeks.

With the failure of this initiative, William Foster took it upon himself to write to C.H. Spurgeon on behalf of the five or six people living in New Brompton who were anxious for a Baptist cause to flourish in their community. (This is a detail recorded in the 'Tabernacle Tidings' for February 1929). Spurgeon's response to this request was to write to James Smith, the Baptist Minister at Zion, Chatham to ask him to take a lead on this matter, and to promise both his interest and support in the new venture.

On November 15th 1878 Rev James Smith called a meeting with his deacons at Zion "relative to the opening of a branch church at New Brompton." James Smith had arrived at Chatham from Woolwich in June 1875 and had an amazingly fruitful ministry baptizing in the region of 100 people in his first three years. He informed the meeting that Spurgeon was willing to supply the ministry in New Brompton for six months free of all charge. A working committee was formed consisting of the deacons of Zion, Chatham and three members residing at New Brompton. Mr John Webb would serve as Treasurer and Mr Foster as Secretary. The Workmen's Hall was again hired for public worship on 24th November for a period of six months. The Workmen's Hall was just behind no.34 High Street and was accessed by a rather narrow and dark passage way.

By April 1879 things were going well. An application was submitted to Rev Smith from those members of Zion Baptist Church worshipping in New Brompton, requesting that they be allowed to withdraw their membership to form a church in New Brompton. Consequently on April 27th 1879 James Smith officially extended the right hand of fellowship to eighteen founder members of New Brompton Baptist Church. The church was formed on the basis of "the principles commonly held by Particular Baptist Churches, which believe in the doctrine of Particular Redemption, restrict membership to those who have professed faith in the Lord Jesus Christ by baptism, but welcome all believers to the Lord's Table." Of those eighteen founder members, seven were from Zion Baptist Church, Chatham; four were from Woolwich; two from Portsmouth (Landport); three from Meopham, London and Hampshire respectively; and two, Mary Foster and Rachel Rockett, from Enon, Chatham. Present at the founding of the church in April 1879 were two students from Pastors' College, London, Mr F.E. Blackaby and Mr W.W. Blocksidge.

Blackaby and Blocksidge were referred to as "Siamese twins" at College. Spurgeon had singled the two men out and sent them down to New Brompton, taking the services on alternate Sundays. Blocksidge's first Sunday at the Workmen's Hall was 1st December 1878. Once the church was officially formed the two men took turns in chairing Church Meetings. Blackaby was in the chair in July 1879 when a committee of management was formed with William Foster as Treasurer and James William Nearn as Secretary. Mr Blackaby mentioned the desirability of starting a building fund and enquired how much people would be willing to contribute. On Monday 23rd June 1879 a baptismal service was held over at Zion, Chatham with Blocksidge conducting the devotional part and Blackaby immersing the ten candidates. Blocksidge presided at the Lord's Supper on 1st September and received the candidates into membership. Blocksidge was chairing the meeting in October 1879 at which Mr Foster informed them of some land available to purchase on Green Street. The decision to buy this land was referred back to Mr Spurgeon. A second baptismal service was held at Chatham on Monday evening 22nd March 1880 at which seven candidates were immersed. They were subsequently received into membership on 4th May.

Not everything, however, went smoothly in those early days. A dispute arose in April 1880 regarding the use of fermented or unfermented (non-alcoholic) wine at Communion. Tempers were frayed, and at one point Mr Nearn offered his resignation. Mr Blocksidge was called upon to chair a Church Meeting to resolve the conflict, and on June 2nd a ballot was taken at which twelve people voted for the use of fermented wine and seventeen for unfermented. There was one abstention. The matter was allowed to rest. On Tuesday evening 8th June a further nine people from New Brompton were baptised at Zion and were received into membership on 1st August.

Blackaby and Blocksidge appended their names to an undated fund raising appeal that was sent out at this time to the wider Baptist constituency. They described themselves as "co-workers at New Brompton and students at the Pastors' College." The appeal described the initiative of James Smith at Zion, and the growing needs of the town. They had bought some land, the letter stated, and now needed funds to construct a building. The letter ended: "We appeal with confidence to the friends of the working classes and to those who desire to promote the preaching of the gospel and the education of the young."

The Church Meeting minutes from December 14th 1880 record that "Some conversation then ensued respecting making an extra effort on behalf of the ministry with a view, if possible, of securing the services of Mr Blocksidge." By this time Mr Blackaby was already in the frame for the pastorate at Stow on the Wold which he commenced in 1881. Blackaby returned to Medway in 1898 when he took over at Zion, Chatham for five years, after which he made several guest appearances at Gillingham before his retirement in 1923. But it was Blocksidge who seemed earmarked for New Brompton, the only problem for the fledgling church being how to afford him. Their income was limited and they were already raising funds for a building. Once again it was Charles Haddon Spurgeon who came to the rescue. At the Church Meeting on March 8th 1881 it was reported that Mr Spurgeon had offered to pay £50 a year for the first year and £25 a year for the second year if the church were willing to take him on. In the face of such generosity the church unanimously offered the pastorate to Mr Blocksidge, thirty members being present. On 19th April Mr Nearn read to the meeting Blocksidge's letter of acceptance, and in June the church wrote to Spurgeon expressing their immense gratitude for his kindness and generosity.

Spurgeon's generosity was not limited to the cause at New Brompton. In several new churches in the South of England, including Rochester, Spurgeon made significant personal contributions to the stipends of the first pastors. In the case of New Brompton, however, Spurgeon was to go even further and provide the lion's share of the money for the new building itself. The 1881 building on Green Street occupied the rear of the present site and was 56 feet long and 20 feet wide. It served as Sunday School and as a place of worship, and cost in the region of £700. The Stone Laying was on 21st September 1881 and the building was opened on November 8th. Towards this project Spurgeon contributed a massive £145.

Spurgeon was to make a further gift of £50 towards the Tabernacle when it was being constructed seven years later. His generosity was followed by that of George Hambrook Dean of Sittingbourne Baptist Church. Mr Dean contributed £72 to the building of the first Green Street premises and he was to make further donations over the next twenty years. Dean's munificence was again felt throughout the Kent and Sussex Baptist Association which he served as Treasurer from 1882 – 1925. Numerous church building schemes were recipients of financial support from Mr G.H. Dean. His name, or the name of his wife and daughter, appear on several foundation stones of Baptist Church buildings which were constructed at this period.

Blocksidge chaired his first Church Meeting as pastor in July 1881. His Recognition Service took place in the August with the College Principal, Rev D. Gracey delivering the charge to the minister while Rev James Smith of Zion, Chatham gave the charge to the church. The church generously offered Mr Blocksidge five days holiday per year as part of his terms of settlement. Blocksidge felt sure he wouldn't need to take them all!

The Sunday School was inaugurated on Sunday 1st January 1882. Blocksidge's own recollections are recorded in the 'Tabernacle Tidings' for April 1932 in celebration of the fifty years of the Sunday School. Blocksidge recorded that on the first Sunday there were 78 scholars, 40 boys and 38 girls. By 1885 the number had grown to 315. The first Superintendent was James Nearn, the Secretary was Sergeant P. Phillips, and the Treasurer Mr J.H. Cox. There were 37 teachers in 1885. Mr Nearn found combining roles as Sunday School Superintendent and Church Secretary too much, so his brother, Edward, took over as Superintendent for a period. He was succeeded by Mr R.H. Andrews, the Assistant Engineer in the Dockyard. Mr Blocksidge recorded that when the number of children attending the old building on Green Street exceeded eleven hundred then Mr P. Hammond generously built a gallery at the end of the School and put two rooms underneath giving increased accommodation. There was considerable disquiet when it was eventually decided that this old building had to come down to make way for the Tab.. Affection for the old place was very strong. In the end people were somewhat placated by the knowledge that much of the brick and stonework of the old building would be incorporated into the construction of the Tab..

The Blocksidge family moved into 26 Green Street. This was their own property, the church having no manse. Blocksidge was a mature student and had worked in a successful jewellery business in Birmingham before sensing a call to train for the Christian ministry. He was born on 23rd September 1850. His mother died when he was seven and his father when he was twelve. He was profoundly influenced by the ministry of Rev Charles Vince at Graham Street Baptist Church, Birmingham, and it was through that church that he became a Christian, an active church worker, and was finally sent to train for the ministry. He arrived at Spurgeon's College in August 1878. By this time he had married Jane Elizabeth Bickerton (1874). They had their first son, Ernest, in 1875, and their second son, Frank, in 1877. The Blocksidges had a daughter, Florence Jane, in 1879. By the time of the 1881 Census, while Walter was still enrolled as a student at Spurgeon's, the Blocksidge family (mother, two sons and one daughter) were living at 99 Mann Street, Newington. Walter himself was absent when the Census was taken, and there is a record of someone fitting his description living at West Malling as a temporary resident.

The final member of the Blocksidge family was another daughter, Jane, who was born on 3rd January 1883. She lived for just sixteen hours. Her cause of death was recorded as 'debility'. The Blocksidge's grief was to be compounded later that same year when on 20th November 1883 little Florence also died aged four. The cause of death was recorded as 'Pyelitis convulsions'. Walter Blocksidge had been present at the death of both his daughters that year.

Whatever personal agonies the pastor was experiencing at this time there is nothing at all recorded in the church minutes. Instead the work of the church went on apace. The chief project at this time was fund raising for the new Tabernacle. After what must have been a relatively short period of time the building on Green Street was already too small to accommodate all the worshippers, and they were back to meeting in the Public Hall, on the corner of the High Street and Gardiner Street. The Green Street premises were now used for the youth work and Sunday School and a variety of society meetings throughout the week.

One of the most effective fund raising events the church employed was the 'Bazaar'. These were extremely well planned (often themed) events which engaged large numbers of the ladies from the church in sewing, baking, and providing stalls for the eager Gillingham public. The proceeds from these bazaars were colossal. The 1883 Bazaar, for example, raised £120. 11. 9d. The October 1887 Bazaar raised £138.9.6d. But the Bazaar held in October 1885 managed to raise the sum of £207.17.9 which was a staggering 5% of the total cost of the Tabernacle in 1888. It was a four day event which was opened on the first day by Admiral Watson, Superintendent of the Chatham Dockyard.

Personal gifts and donations are again listed in a Building Fund Account book. C.H. Spurgeon and G.H. Dean feature prominently. But R.H. Andrews from HM Dockyard, Chatham, and Sunday School Superintendent, also features regularly as a benefactor to the work of the church.

An extraordinary feature of this period was a national fund raising programme launched by Mr Blocksidge. Between the first week of November 1884 and the first week of December over forty donations were received from all over the country totalling £54. The lion's share of these donations, 29 of them, came from Mr Blocksidge's old stamping ground of Birmingham. During the first half of 1885 more donations came in from Reading, Brighton, Hawkhurst, Norwich, Ramsgate, Cardiff, Sandwich, London, and a dozen from Gravesend. This was an invaluable level of support nationally at a time when several other churches and causes were all bidding for financial assistance.

Annual choir concerts were another source of fund raising, the one in May 1887 raising just over £20. In 1888 Spurgeon himself was happy to have his name attached to another national fund raising brochure for the new Tabernacle. Produced just after the Stone Laying of the new building in July 1888, Spurgeon endorsed the campaign saying there could not be a more deserving cause. The New Brompton people needed a further £2,000 to finance the new building. "Wealthy friends", said Spurgeon, "could not better use their Lord's money than in helping this church at this moment."

The strength of the relationship between Blocksidge and Spurgeon can be gauged from the tone and content of three letters from Spurgeon to his protégé that came into the church's possession in 1992. The first one, dated November 7th 1883 begins, "Dear Mr Blocksidge, I have written Mr Wills [the architect] as you desired and will let you know when he replies." This is further confirmation of Spurgeon's direct involvement in the building scheme. The letter goes on to say, "I always understand you. You have my fullest esteem and perfect confidence. You are my joy and comfort..."

The second letter, dated April 26th 1886, is simply a request for Blocksidge to be prepared to make a short speech at a meeting they were both attending. The third letter, however, dated June 19th 1888, is far more revealing. The letter is to the church rather than to the minister. "Dear friends, I thank you heartily for your earnest loving resolution sent to me by telegram. God bless you." It would appear to be his response to the church's acknowledgement of one of his generous donations to the new building which was in process of being constructed. The letter, however, goes on in a very moving way to describe Spurgeon's opinion of Mr Blocksidge.

"Your esteemed pastor is one of a thousand and deserves from you abounding love and kindness. The more I see of him the more I esteem him. I doubt not he has gathered about him a people like himself."

Given the number of men Spurgeon had trained and with whom he had regular dealings, these warm and effusive comments make clear the very high regard in which Blocksidge was held by the great preacher.

1.   'A History of Gillingham' - Philip Rogers 1947
2.   'The Gillingham Chronicles' p.240 – Ronald Baldwin 1998
3.   'The Gillingham Chronicles' p.240 – Ronald Baldwin 1998
4.   'Chats about Gillingham' p.204 – C.S. Leeds 1906

CHAPTER 2

MR BLOCKSIDGE AND THE TAB

The plans for the new building did not run smoothly. An initial design by the architect, Mr Wills from the Victoria Chambers, Derby, was rejected. This would have provided ground floor access to the worship area. The revised plan elevated the worship area to the first floor leaving the downstairs for classrooms for the Sunday School. The anecdotal story was that Mr Blocksidge believed that the church was built on the Sunday School, and that this should be reflected in the design of the building.

During 1886 and 1887, however, a far more fundamental problem emerged to derail the building plans. On August 28th 1886 Mr Blocksidge wrote to all the church members inviting them to attend a Special Church Meeting on 2nd September at which the pastor wished to lay out an alternative proposal. At the meeting Mr Blocksidge read out a proposal for "procuring a new site for the proposed chapel, and spoke in high terms of the site as proposed by your committee, situated on the other side of the railway near the station." The specific site is not identified and details of the conversations at the meeting were not recorded, save for the phrase, "a long discussion ensued". The meeting was adjourned until the 7th September whereupon Mr Blocksidge again "explained the great desirability of procuring a new site, speaking at some length on the advantage of the one as proposed by the committee." The recommendation was put to the meeting: "Shall we procure a new site for our proposed chapel?" The voting in favour of the motion was 131, against 27, and there were 3 abstentions.

Throughout 1886 and 1887 the church continued to meet for worship in the Public Hall. But the question of whether to purchase this new site was still not fully resolved in spite of the vote of September 7th. A printed letter dated May 5th 1887 urged members to attend another Special Church Meeting on 11th May where a very definite decision about the new site needed to be taken. Alas! The minutes of that meeting were never entered into the Minute Book and the page is blank! This seems slightly more than an oversight, and one wonders if the pastor was reluctant to let posterity into the discussion that took place on that occasion. Suffice to say, the

Church Meeting held on May 25th 1887 began: "Pastor stated that he had written to Mr Ball declining to purchase the site of land on the other side of the railway."

In May 1888 tenders were put out on Mr Wills' revised building plan for the new chapel and schoolrooms. The quote that was accepted was for £3298 and was from Messrs Naylor & Son of Rochester. The church agreed to borrow £2,000 in order to finance the building work. That same month the original Schoolroom on Green Street was demolished.

The Stone Laying ceremony took place on 19th July 1888. Several stones were laid including ones by the High Constables of Chatham and Gillingham; Mrs G.H. Dean and Pastor W.W. Blocksidge; and one by Mr C.F. Allison. He was one of the deacons of the Metropolitan Tabernacle, thereby maintaining a link with Spurgeon's own church. This perpetuated a tradition that had developed over the years where leaders connected with the Metropolitan Tabernacle were present at Stone Laying ceremonies of churches where Spurgeon had some direct interest or involvement. In addition to the stones that were laid on 19th July there was one that was re-laid. A stone that was laid in the original building on September 21st 1881 by Miss Marian Dean of Sittingbourne was re-laid in the ground floor entrance of the new Tabernacle, establishing some physical and tangible connection with the old meeting place.

In August 1888, one month after the Stone Laying ceremony, Mr Blocksidge was again in some considerable anxiety. The Church Meeting that month had fifty out of two hundred members in attendance, and he feared that this indicated an insufficient level of support from the membership. Unless they rallied together behind the project, "the building that was being erected would be but a monument of their folly." "Who", said Mr Blocksidge, "feels confident of signing for £2,000 worth of loans without feeling the confidence of the people on whose behalf he is signing." Last minute nerves are often part of any building scheme, but in the end a vote of the male members of the church did approve a loan of £2,000 with the London and County Bank.

The Opening Services took place on Wednesday 30th January 1889. In the afternoon Rev Charles Spurgeon of Greenwich (son of C.H. Spurgeon) preached despite his "prostrate state of health". His text was from 1Corinthians 2:2, "I determined to know nothing among you except Jesus Christ and Him crucified." Five hundred friends sat down to tea following the afternoon service. This was the preliminary for the evening meeting. On Sunday 3rd February, on what should have been Blocksidge's moment of triumph, the services were conducted by Rev F.E. Blackaby. The Church Meeting minutes record that, "The pastor's voice having failed he was deprived of the power and pleasure of expressing the desires that filled his mind on such an interesting occasion." Blocksidge did manage to baptise eight people during the afternoon service, but the following Sunday evening Mr Nearn, the Church Secretary, had to inform a hastily convened Church Meeting that "Our pastor's health having completely broken down, and his medical advisor having recommended entire rest and change ... [the deacons advise]... that our pastor go away to Ilfracombe, Devonshire, and that four weeks salary be paid him in advance." The proposal was agreed unanimously, and church members were invited to make separate gifts to the Blocksidges should they wish to do so. In order to relieve the pastor of any financial anxieties the church agreed to increase his salary from £2. 10 shillings a week to £3 a week on 30th April 1889.

Mr Blocksidge was back at Green Street by April that year, but he was to suffer a further bout of ill health in 1893. The church's report to the Kent and Sussex Baptist Association for 1894 informed the churches that in September 1893 Blocksidge had been taken seriously ill while conducting the evening service, although they were relieved to report that he was now (in 1894) back with strength and vigour.

The new building brought with it issues that needed to be addressed. How should the weekly offerings be collected? By a plate being passed round it was decided. How should we agree who sits where in the new chapel? By a system of pew rents it was decided. Families could purchase a pew for the year. Visitors could only occupy that pew if the family concerned had not taken up possession by the time of the first hymn. One could imagine numerous arguments breaking out if the person who paid for the pew turned up late and found someone already sitting in it. In such situations the role of the seat steward was a very important one, and seat stewards were elected annually in order that they might have the confidence of the people. An early indication of the congregational strength at this time can be gleaned from a minute of the Deacons Meeting on 9th April 1889. It recommended that because all pews were already filled in the Tabernacle, then extra chairs should be placed at the end of the rows "for the accommodation of strangers".

The building was registered for the solemnization of marriages in 1890.

Inevitably there were teething problems with the new building and its organisation. Mr Blocksidge had to handle very delicate situations around temperamental musicians. The harmonium player resigned in July 1889 and the choirmaster also resigned at the same time. But the greatest challenge facing Mr Blocksidge was reported to the Church Meeting on 7th August 1889: "Our pastor stated that a serious rumour was in circulation to the effect that he had appropriated money from the Building Fund to purchase a piano for himself."

The deacons set out at once to investigate the rumour. A formal enquiry was launched under brother R.H. Andrews, and an interim report was issued on 13th August which exonerated the pastor. They had examined all expenditure between 1883 and 1889 and found nothing out of place. The deacons intended, however, to try and trace the source of the rumour which meant that their final report was not issued until 7th October. They concluded that the rumour had arisen from a misunderstanding over a half heard conversation. No malice had been intended, and of course, no basis was ever found to the rumour. "The character of our pastor has not in the slightest been injured." Nevertheless it must have been a very stressful time for Mr Blocksidge with this cloud of uncertainty hanging over him.

The 1891 Census revealed that the Blocksidges were still living at 26 Green Street. Walter (aged 40 last birthday) and his wife, Jane Elizabeth, (42 last birthday) shared the house with their two sons, Ernest, aged 15 and Frank, aged 13, and a domestic servant named Lilian Card (or Curd) aged 16. Lilian was born in New Brompton but her name does not correspond with any similar name on the Church Members Roll. Her job in the household would have been to provide support for Mrs Blocksidge.

In February 1892 the deacons resolved "to hold two special services in connection with the great loss the Christian Church had sustained by the death of Mr C.H. Spurgeon." Spurgeon's demise created one urgent and practical problem for New Brompton Baptist Church in that Spurgeon had served as Treasurer to their Building Fund. A replacement was needed, and in the March Mr Featherby was appointed to the role.

An extensive house to house visitation scheme was launched in 1892 trying to ascertain whether those moving into the area attended any place of worship. There is also reference in the deacons' minutes at this time to an "Old Brompton Mission" for which Green Street had some responsibility.

On 14th November 1894 there is a very interesting entry in the Deacons Meeting minutes: "A numerously signed memorial of the townspeople including the signatures of the four resident Non-Conformist ministers, asking our pastor to allow himself to be nominated as candidate for District Councillor was then read to the brethren." Mr Blocksidge allowed his candidacy to go forward to the townspeople with the result that he was duly elected a District Councillor, his name topping the poll. In his first ever (1895) New Year's Letter to the members of the church and congregation Mr Blocksidge mentioned his election and the new responsibilities he would be taking on. He asked the church for its support. "I take the work looking to God for strength and guidance, and looking to you to help me while serving you and the town upon the council."

Mr Blocksidge threw himself into local politics with relish. Even prior to his election he had made a foray into the world of local education. Such was the strength of the Non-Conformist Churches in Medway at this time that they produced their own magazine, "The Local Messenger" (subtitled, 'the organ of the Non-Conformist churches of Chatham, Rochester, Strood, Brompton and District'). The September 1893 edition carried on page ii a biography of Blocksidge under the heading, 'Local workers and their work.' But the following two pages were taken up with an article by Blocksidge entitled "A few brief reasons why Gillingham ought to have a School Board." Blocksidge's argument was that there were insufficient school places for the children of the town and that a new school should be provided by the local authority which was also under local control. "I would advocate the formation of a Board School on the grounds of religious freedom, believing it will be an advantage to the parish to have a school managed independently of any denomination." He went on to argue for this new school "on the grounds of true economy" believing it to be good value for money for the rate payers of New Brompton.

Once elected as District Councillor, Blocksidge's next campaign was for Gillingham to have its own Swimming Baths. A newspaper article dated July 6th 1895 provided coverage of the debate in Council where Mr Blocksidge proposed the adoption of the Baths and Washhouses Act. He maintained that many residents of New Brompton had to travel to Rochester to enjoy swimming, and he felt confident that a town of its size ought to be able to sustain a Swimming Baths of its own. From enquiry in Birmingham and Maidstone he had discovered that Swimming Baths could turn a profit so that this could be of financial benefit to the Council. Blocksidge's fellow councillors were not so convinced. Councillor Bullock did not believe in grandmotherly legislation, and "as custodians of the public pocket they were not prepared to spend money yet on such a scheme." A motion to defer any decision to a later date was approved eight votes to three. The Swimming Baths were not built for several more years. Blocksidge only served one three year term as a Councillor and did not seek re-election.

Throughout the 1890s the church continued to take steps to clear the debt it had taken out on building the Tabernacle. There were more bazaars and other fund raising events. In March 1895 the pastor was again sent to Birmingham to obtain funds to repay the bank. In May the church received a huge boost when Mr Blackaby published an article in the Spurgeonic publication "The Sword and Trowel" (volume xxxi) entitled "our own men and their work". The article provided details of Blocksidge's call to the church and his subsequent ministry, but the ostensible purpose was an unashamed appeal for funds. Blackaby informed the readers that the financially exhausted church still had £900 to repay, and he appealed to some wealthy benefactor of the wider Baptist family to find at least £400 in order to relieve the burden on this hard pressed congregation. Donors should write to Blocksidge at his Green Street address.

By June 1896 the church was able to hold special services for the extinction of the chapel debt. The Chatham News for June 20th gave extensive coverage of the services and at times verbatim coverage of what was said. The Sunday morning services had been led by Mr Blocksidge who drew upon allusions to building the walls of Jerusalem in the time of Nehemiah. The work was only accomplished as the people worked together. A baptismal service was held in the afternoon, and in the evening Rev Blackaby preached. The following Tuesday evening there was a special meeting preceded by Tea. The meeting was chaired by Mr G.H. Dean of Sittingbourne. Mr Dean said that "theirs was a funeral job that day, for they had buried their debt" (laughter and applause). "The Tabernacle was a triumph of voluntaryism." Rev Charles Spurgeon got them to sing "Praise God from whom all blessings flow." He felt that the eyes of his late beloved father would be "beaming with joy as he beheld their gathering that night." Spurgeon said that he was amazed at what the church had been able to achieve in the last seven years with the mountain of debt around them. How much more might they accomplish now that debt had been removed. "For seven years their pastor had worn a worried look" (laughter). Now they could look forward to a change in his countenance. "Now their building was free from debt he would advise them to cram it – to cram it until they become packed in like sardines, or like the periwinkles they had had for tea"(loud laughter). Spurgeon paid special tribute to those who had faithfully contributed to the penny a week scheme.

Mr J.W. Nearn, the Church Secretary, then spoke. He alluded to the flourishing Sunday School which had between 500 – 600 scholars on the books. Mr Nearn then presented Mr Blocksidge with a gold watch, a purse of money, and an album containing the names of the subscribers. He suggested that the Blocksidges might like to purchase a suite of drawing room furniture (loud applause). In making a reply Mr Blocksidge said that he was sure that he did not deserve their gifts ('no' from the congregation). He also thanked them on behalf of his wife. "Her life had been an inspiration to him." Blocksidge was then able to announce that, in keeping with a promise made several years before, he had received a cheque for 100 guineas from Mr George Dean which would extinguish the remaining money owed on the building. The amount now raised was in excess of £4,000.

Rev John Doubleday (Sittingbourne), an old college friend of Blackaby and Blocksidge, who referred to them in their College days as "the Siamese twins", expressed the hope that brother Blocksidge "would put fat on now

17

he was free from anxiety." Mr Blackaby wondered whether as the other half of the Siamese twins he ought to receive half the gifts Blocksidge had been given! Rev G.A. Miller, on behalf of the Rochester and Chatham ministers, suggested that the church might like to buy a manse to accommodate Mr Blocksidge's suite of furniture!

Towards the end of 1896 the church received more good news when they were informed that one of their members, brother Murray, had been received into Pastor's College to train for the ministry. In May 1897 it was another proud moment for the church when they were able to accommodate the Kent and Sussex Baptist Association for their two-day annual meetings. It was a huge undertaking in providing food and hospitality for dozens of delegates from across the region. The church rallied to the occasion admirably. In 1900 Blocksidge was given further recognition when he was elected the Moderator of the Kent & Sussex Baptist Association, an annual appointment but one which was regarded as a mark of distinction and honour.

By this time the church had a new Church Secretary. A Deacons Meeting minute for September 1899 records: "Since our last meeting an event had occurred by which the whole church and congregation had been plunged into mourning. On the evening of 7th August last at St Bartholomew's hospital after a very brief but sharp illness our esteemed and honoured Secretary of the Church, brother J.W. Nearn passed peacefully into the presence of his master." They recorded how Mr Nearn had served not only twenty years as Church Secretary but also at various times, Choirmaster and Sunday School Superintendent. "Our brother's dignified presence will be missed in the church and his counsels in the diaconate." The Church Meeting minutes contain a copy of the letter which Blocksidge sent to Mrs Nearn. It was a very moving letter and contained a glowing tribute to his "long and valuable services" to the church. "His promptitude and accuracy in attending to the business of the church, and his consistent and devoted life have gained our esteem and love." A marble plaque was set up in the church "to perpetuate his memory." Mr W. Albert Dyke was appointed his successor.

Freed from the burden of debt the church felt some liberty in responding to other appeals for money including one from the Metropolitan

18

Tabernacle as well as one from the Kent & Sussex Baptist Association's appeal on behalf of Rochester Baptist Church. But by the autumn of 1899 the church were once again contemplating major capital expenditure. They were looking to purchase the two houses next door to the church (no.2 and no.4 Green Street); an enlargement to the Sunday School; the purchase of an organ; and the installation of electric light and ventilation into the Tab.. The November Church Meeting sanctioned the purchase of the two houses from Mr Robson for £700, and in April 1900 they agreed to purchase an organ from St John's Church, Lewisham for £135. The same meeting agreed for the church to take out loans totalling £1,800 with the London and County Bank at 4% interest, and with this to construct a new building to the rear of the Tab. on the site of the original schoolroom.

The Deacons Meeting minutes for 1900 reveal that the architect, Mr Hammond, was presenting them with far more ambitious plans than they had anticipated with a scheme to create a third floor extension at the rear of the Tab. running to £600 more than they had budgeted. The scheme needed to be cut back. Eventually a design was agreed and the quote of £900 from Mr Langley was accepted for all the new building work. The memorial stones for the schoolroom were laid in September 1900 with Messrs Moffett, Rogers and Blocksidge laying three of the stones, and contributing £50 each for the privilege. It was Mrs Blocksidge's name that actually appeared on the stone laid by her husband.

The organ was installed in November 1900, and a full organ recital was given to mark the occasion. The new classrooms were officially opened on 27th January 1901.

The Census for 1901 reveals that the Blocksidges had now moved house and were living at 12 Balmoral Road which had only recently been built. Walter was again away from home when the census was taken, and this corresponds with the Deacons Meeting minutes which mention his journey to Palestine and Egypt in March of that year. The Baptist Union Handbook indicates that the Blocksidges moved to Balmoral Road during 1897. Present at 12 Balmoral Road on Census day were Jane Blocksidge, aged 51; her son Ernest, aged 25, now a draughtsman at the dockyard; her son Frank, aged 23, a dental assistant; Amelia Chalklin, aged 22, a domestic servant, who was born in Wouldham, Kent; and in addition

19

there was Mary Blocksidge, single, aged 53, who was Mr Blocksidge's sister from Birmingham. Her presence during Walter's absence gives further confirmation of the poor health of Mrs Blocksidge herself. She wasn't able to be left on her own while her husband was away.

In the early years of their ministry at Green Street Mrs Blocksidge appears to have fulfilled a role expected of the minister's wife of those days. In February 1885, for example, her name appears at the head of a list of women of the church organising the tea committee. In May 1894 she conducted a membership interview, along with another female member, for a prospective candidate. In March 1896 she was again heading up the tea committee, but not thereafter. In June 1896, during the service to mark the extinction of the church debt, Mr Dean referred to both Mr and Mrs Blocksidge having been laid very low, "though in His mercy they have been restored to health and strength" (applause). In October 1900 all the deacons' wives names, and several other prominent women in the church, appear on various committee lists, but not Mrs Blocksidge. At the close of the AGM in March 1905, we find what was to become a customary valediction at all subsequent meetings: that "an expression of love and sympathy be sent to Mrs Blocksidge."

In June 1906 Mr Blocksidge celebrated his 25th Anniversary as pastor of the church. Predictably large celebrations were held, but alas Mrs Blocksidge could not be present. It fell to Samuel Strugnell, the Church Treasurer, to make a very eloquent speech on that occasion, during which he made reference to Mrs Blocksidge's incapacity: "That one lying ill and suffering at home had not been forgotten (hear, hear). Very many of the congregation going to call on her took flowers, so the pastor would accept on his wife's behalf a silver epergne in which to display them (applause). What influence Mrs Blocksidge had on their pastor, and through him, on them all, could only be understood by those who knew her. Though her afflictions prevented her from sharing her husband's joy and his work among them she was never forgotten and she was loved by all (applause)."

The precise nature of Mrs Blocksidge's chronic condition was never made clear. Her husband rarely made mention of anything of a personal nature. The only exception to this appears in his New Year's letter for 1911: "My own spirit has found great comfort, and my dear wife wonderful support, in the happy consciousness of the deep sympathy of our beloved people in our time of domestic pain. The dear invalid would like to express her thanks for the generous, loving, Christian sympathy and constant prayers of the members of the church and congregation. Accept our united thanks for your valuable and successful intercession on our behalf."

The 1911 Census reveals that the Blocksidges had again moved house, this time to 122 Balmoral Road. Both the boys had left home and Mrs Blocksidge was assisted by a 'Lady's help' called Frances Angel Loft. She was single, and aged 38. There is a lady of that same name who became a member at Green Street in 1889.

Mrs Blocksidge continued in her chronic condition until January 23rd 1925 when she died aged 76. The death was registered by her daughter-in-law, Ethel Blocksidge, who lived at 12 Balmoral Road, and the cause of death was recorded as "osteo-arthritis" and "influenza asthenia". The doctor completing the certificate also indicated that Mrs Blocksidge was "bedridden".

The Blocksidge boys both became church members. Ernest was baptised in September 1895. He married a young lady from the church, Henrietta Lilian Bloor, on 26th June 1901. Two years later the couple had their membership transferred to Hither Green Baptist Church, London. Frank Blocksidge was baptised in 1898 and became quite involved in the life of the church. He sang a solo at the end of the Church Meeting in November 1898, and was elected a seat steward in October 1899. He married a young woman from the church, Ethel Sophia Hyde Nicholson, in 1907. She was the church organist's daughter. Curiously, the Church Membership Roll has a note indicating that the couple were not married in the Tab.. Frank Blocksidge continued his duties as seat steward until resigning in March 1912 because "professional duties" prevented him from attending regularly. During the First World War he saw active service in France, Mesopotamia and Palestine. He remained on the Church Members Roll until his name was removed in October 1934.

Mr Blocksidge's Silver Jubilee celebrations, already referred to, were covered extensively in the 'Gillingham Observer' for June 1906. They record the pastor's text on the first Sunday in June, Deuteronomy 8:2,

21

"And thou shalt remember all the ways which the Lord thy God led thee." Mention is made of the Mayor of Gillingham's remarks at the mid week service in which he referred to Blocksidge as a Bishop among the town's Non-Conformists. The Mayor's suggestion that the church might wish to provide a seat in the newly created Gillingham Park, in recognition of their pastor's Silver Jubilee, was taken up by the church. It was duly presented to the Park in July.

The main speaker at the Pastor's Silver Jubilee celebrations was Mr Strugnell, the Church Treasurer. In addition to the very kindly comments made with regard to Mrs Blocksidge, Mr Strugnell took the opportunity to have some fun at the pastor's expense. He said that they had all been at the receiving end from Mr Blocksidge, well now the tables were turned and it was payback time (laughter). "Nemesis had overtaken him" (loud laughter). Strugnell presented Mr Blocksidge with an illuminated and framed address which listed his fine qualities and their appreciation of him. Strugnell also presented the pastor with a purse of gold "which (Mr Strugnell said) having regard to the pastor's weakness for giving away all the money he could get hold of, ought to be sent to Mrs Blocksidge" (applause and laughter). "The pastor was a good Prime Minister, but a poor Chancellor of the Exchequer" (laughter).

CHAPTER 3

GROWTH, DEVELOPMENT AND THE NEW MISSIONS

The most accurate measure of the size of a Baptist Church comes from the church membership figures which are submitted to the Baptist Union and which appear in the annual BU Handbook. These figures can only give a trend as to what was taking place in the life of the church, and cannot provide us with an accurate picture of congregational strength. This is particularly the case with a church such as New Brompton Baptist Church which practised closed membership, and only allowed into membership those who had been baptised as believers and by immersion. In such a flourishing and popular church there would have been a number of worshippers from other church traditions who never felt able to come into membership. This was only recognised in 1917 when a separate communicant roll was established for those who were recognised as part of the worshipping community but who were not formally in church membership.

There were 18 people who on 27th April 1879 became Founder Members of New Brompton Baptist Church. By the time Mr Blocksidge had been inducted as pastor of the church the membership figure had grown to 56, and two years later was 129. The table and graph below give a clear indication of the growth of the church membership at this period, reaching its peak in 1904 when there were 449 members.

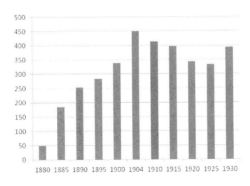

The Church Membership Roll indicates clearly that a large majority of these members came through baptism. In the first twenty five years of the church (1879 - 1904) there were 401 baptisms at an average of slightly over 16 per year. Some years were quite prolific. In 1885 there were 41 baptisms. In 1889 there were 42 baptisms. In 1901 there were 45 baptisms. These were heady days, and one can discern the energy and excitement that must have come through these expressions of faith and commitment.

But a feature of New Brompton Baptist Church was the large number of people who joined the church on transfer from other Baptist Churches. Chatham and Gillingham were growing areas, and the dockyard was providing employment for large numbers of workers. At a time when the Baptist denomination was very strong in industrial areas, many of those coming to the area for work sought to join a local Baptist Church. In that same twenty five year period, therefore (1879 – 1904), there were 238 people who joined the membership on transfer from other Baptist Churches.

By extending the period under investigation to 1930 (the first fifty two years of the church's history), the trends become much clearer. During that period 1,305 people became church members of whom 441 or 33.79% were transfers from other churches. Of these a significant number came from the local area. Approximately 61 people transferred from Zion, Chatham which had quite a turbulent history. A further 95 people came from Kent; with Sittingbourne, Sheerness and Canterbury accounting for over a third of these. There were 87 people who came from London, with Woolwich being quite a popular place of origin. Finally, there were 61 people from Wales of whom over half transferred, not surprisingly, from the Baptist Church at Pembroke Dock.

The Church Membership Roll also reveals something of the fluidity and mobility of the population. Assumptions about communities being more stable and static in those days are not borne out by the evidence. Between 1879 and 1930 there were 269 people who were transferred ('dismissed' is the word usually used) to other churches. Of these 8 were transferred to Pembroke Dock, 11 to Woolwich and a further 11 to Devonport. There were 12 members who transferred to Rochester, and 13 who went to Portsmouth. Surprisingly there were also a large number of members who emigrated. William and Mary Foster, two of the founder members of the church, went to Australia, while John and Ellen Webb, numbers 4&5 on the Church Roll, moved to the USA in 1885. Other members also moved to Australia and the USA, while others went to Ireland, India, Canada and South Africa.

Perhaps one of the most disappointing features of the church membership statistics were the number of people who were deleted from the Church Roll for non-attendance. In February 1895 there were 28 names deleted from the Church Roll. In December 1904 there were 38 more names deleted. In February 1912 the 'Gillingham Observer' carried an article about the 23rd Anniversary of the opening of the Tab.. The event also marked a presentation to Mr Strugnell, the Church Treasurer, and his wife, who were moving to Southsea to be nearer their family. The newspaper article provided details of the Annual Report presented by Mr Dyke, the Church Secretary. He reported that there were 413 members, over 1,000 Sunday School scholars, and 80 Teachers. He also admitted that 116 names had so far been deleted from the Church Roll for non-attendance.

Over the years this was a trend that increased significantly and perhaps indicates something of the weak pastoral care structure as the church grew in size. The pastoral oversight when the church had 50 members did not work so well when the same church had 400 members. Mr Dyke did offer one crumb of comfort from these disappointing statistics. Of the 116 names deleted for non-attendance only 20 had joined the church through baptism. The remaining 96 names were of people who had transferred in from other churches. The implication was that the Christian commitment of those who came from other churches was not as strong as those 'home grown' converts. Looking at this another way: perhaps those coming from other parts of the country found it difficult to feel they belonged in the midst of people they did not really know.

With the rapid growth of the congregation and the church membership there came a demand for auxiliary organisations to support the interests, and occupy the time, of the large number of people who would have found few other distractions in late Victorian and early Edwardian England. The Temperance (teetotalism) movement was big business in Non-Conformist circles, and Green Street was no exception. A thriving Band of Hope was formed with Mr Blocksidge as its President[1]. A Bible Reading Association was formed which had considerable support from people within the church. A Christian Endeavour was also formed which was to provide huge social and spiritual support for generations of young people. Interestingly though, persistent requests to form a Scout Troop were always turned down.

In 1919 the growth of the church required an expansion of the leadership team, and two further places were created on the diaconate.

With the Green Street building bulging at the seams, the only other way for expansion was to explore auxiliary Missions. These were satellite congregations often set up in parts of the community geographically removed from the centre. This was a very common practice in Baptist Churches. Zion, Chatham for example reported to the Association in 1894 the success of their Mission station at Blue Bell Hill which had opened the previous year and was now free of debt. At the same time they were running Missions at Borstal and Luton Road. By 1902 Zion were boasting of starting a cottage Mission in the village of Walderslade, and were persevering with a Mission in a very difficult part of Chatham called Hardstown. The Baptist Church in Rochester made reference to its Mission in Frindsbury when it reported to the Association in 1914.

The first reference to a Mission associated with Gillingham Baptist Church is in the Deacons minutes for October 1892 when mention is made of the "Old Brompton Mission Hall". A favourable report received by the deacons in the November of that year persuaded them to retain the Mission for the next twelve months. It is possible that in its first phase the cause at Old Brompton may have been independent because in March 1903 a deputation from the Old Brompton Mission met the deacons to ask the Green Street Church to take the work over. The deacons responded favourably to this request, and at the Church Meeting in April 1903 it was agreed "that the Old Brompton Mission be taken over as a Baptist Mission in connection with the Tabernacle."

In April 1908 there is reference to both the Old Brompton Mission and the Pier Road Mission. There were issues surrounding financing the two satellites, and a committee from the diaconate and the Missions was formed to see what could be done. In January 1912 a Male Voice Choir

Concert was held in aid of the Old Brompton and Pier Road Missions. From Mr Blocksidge's own recollections in the 'Tabernacle Tidings' for April 1932, the cause at Pier Road Mission and Old Brompton Mission was very much the work of the older Sunday School scholars and their teachers.

The 1913 Report to the Kent and Sussex Association explained the demise of the Old Brompton Mission. Having expressed their thanks to God for the increase and growth of the congregation at the Tab. the Report went on to say: "We have one cause for sincere regret – our Mission held for 16 years in Old Brompton in a building that had been used as a church and Masonic Hall was condemned as insecure, and by the order of the corporation was demolished. This has scattered the teachers and the scholars; they have no place in which to meet."

This is not quite the whole story. At a Church Meeting on 1st October 1913 Mr Richard Jewell put forward a proposal to purchase a new site for the Old Brompton Mission. The proposal was defeated by 32 votes to 29.

The Pier Road Mission, however, did survive. In November 1916 the Superintendent of the Pier Road Mission requested a meeting with the deacons. A similar request was made in May 1917. At the Deacons Meeting in May 1919 it was reported that a new Hall had become available which would be suitable for the Pier Road Mission. The owners were asking £175 for it, but the deacons agreed to offer £150. In June this offer was accepted, and in July it was insured for £500. During October 1919 a meeting took place between the deacons at the Tab. and representatives from the Mission, along with Mr French, an architect. It was recognised that the building would need upgrading to be fit for purpose. Unfortunately, the estimate from the architect was between £900 and £1,000. It was decided that this was too much to spend; that temporary repairs only should be made and that a new venue for the Mission be found. The same month (October 1919) the Church Meeting minutes record that a meeting of the officers, teachers and workers of Pier Road Mission came forward with a recommendation to purchase a piece of land either on Camden Road or Milner Road ("The former for preference") "for the purpose of erecting a Mission Hall to be known as the 'Gillingham Baptist War Memorial Hall.'" In February 1920 the church were pleased to sell the building on

Pier Road for £150, and to cut their losses. In April 1920 they agreed to buy a plot of land on Camden Road. Two of the deacons, brother Woods and brother Fieldgate, provided loans of £500 each to allow the purchase to take place. In June 1920 the Church Meeting agreed to purchase a hut from Fort Pitt to be relocated on the Camden Road site. A bank loan was taken out to cover the cost. This asbestos hut had been used in World War 1 as a Canadian Military Hospital.

The Church Meeting on 23rd March 1921 approved detailed rules for the maintenance and management of the Baptist Memorial Hall, Camden Road, including the commencement of a Band of Hope. Brother Neill was appointed the first Superintendent. In April it was reported at the Deacons Meeting that the Fire Insurance Policy for Camden Road Hall would be kept in the church safe. On 18th May 1921 the official opening of the Camden Road Mission took place.

Mr Blocksidge's interest in the developments of the Camden Road Mission can be gauged through his New Year Letters. Writing to the church and congregation on New Year's Day 1920 he reminded them of the sacrifices they would need to make to erect a new Mission Hall to accommodate the Pier Road Mission Sunday School. The building would also conduct religious services, preach the Gospel, and educate the young in the principles of Jesus Christ. His 1921 New Year Letter mentioned the brass War Memorial being fixed in the Tab. which would list the names of the twenty young men who had fallen during the late war. However, "the larger Memorial is now being erected which we hope will be completed about the middle of February." It is "our War Memorial Hall in Camden Road" which will serve as church and Sunday School in that part of the neighbourhood where there is no Non-Conformist church.

The Camden Road Mission had a somewhat bumpy start. The Church Meeting on September 22nd 1922 mentioned that "certain difficulties have arisen at the Mission." The pastor explained what he had done "to bring about a peaceful settlement." Mr Neill resigned as Superintendent of the Mission, and in April 1923 brother Carter was appointed in his place. For the next seventy years the Camden Road Mission was to act as a satellite congregation of Green Street, and was to feature regularly in the life of the church, its debates and meetings. In 1927 following Mr Carter's resignation the position of Superintendent was given to Richard Jewell.

There was great significance and poignancy for the Gillingham Church that Camden Road should serve as a War Memorial. The First World War had an impact on the town and the churches in a way that is hard for us to comprehend today.

After war broke out in 1914 the Tab. became a very different place. Dark blinds were fitted to all the windows. The church opened up the schoolrooms on week nights (August 1914) for new military recruits to use for recreational purposes. This was reported in the Baptist Times for 2nd October 1914. The article also mentioned that Mr Blocksidge was deputy chaplain to the forces. Very soon (May 1915) plans were in place to provide tea on Sunday afternoon for soldiers and sailors. This continued throughout the duration of the war. The church's report to the Association in 1915 mentioned that the Sunday School was deprived of almost all the male teachers who were obliged to go to duty on Sunday in the dockyard. From the end of 1917 the Tab. was hosting special Parade Services on Sundays for the troops.

The most interesting and moving information regarding the impact of the war on the church community is found in Mr Blocksidge's New Year's Day letters. In 1915 he referred to the fact that the previous year had been "overshadowed by war". But he maintained, "We humbly believe that God's blessing will rest upon our endeavours in the cause of righteousness, and that our children, the nations of Europe, and the world will gain a clearer view of truth, honour and purity."

The 1916 letter reflects a more prolonged exposure to conflict. He expresses pleasure in the past year at being able to cater for 2,500 soldiers on Sunday afternoons during the summer months. But he also gives space to express sympathy to those who lost loved ones during the year. "We would especially desire the comfort of God for those whose brave sons have answered the call of king and country, and in their defence have made the great and supreme sacrifice."

The 1917 letter betrays a real war weariness. "Every institution and organisation has felt the depressing effect of the war." He extended thoughts and prayers for those serving overseas. (Mr Nicholson, the church organist, for example, went to the front in January 1917). But Mr Blocksidge also gave consideration to "the men who have thronged our Rest Room, and from the trenches and battlefields, from camps and barracks, letters come from these brave men. From churches, grateful parents, wives and families, letters are sent thanking us for our care of those who are away from their home and social associations." Many of these men have gone on to die in the battlefields. "We have gripped their hands, looked into their eyes, and heard their grateful thanks."

In his 1918 New Year letter Mr Blocksidge referred to the church Rest Room as a "home away from home." He noted with pleasure and pride how many soldiers "have seen a new vision of Christianity, and have come on Sunday to worship with the people who have treated them kindly during the week." Reading those annual letters and the space he gave to the effect of the war, it is almost as if the pastor himself was being changed; his horizons were being expanded; and he found a new purpose and significance in meeting raw human need. "How eagerly we desire to see this terrible war brought to a conclusion." "Every phase of life is affected, the health of the people suffers, minds are restless, and hearts are sad." He even called upon his readers to exercise self denial and limit their food intake for the sake of the war effort.

Predictably the tone of his 1919 letter, coming a matter of weeks after the end of hostilities, was jubilant. He gave thanks to God that "the dark forces of evil" had been defeated. He looked forward to a time when "the forces of justice, liberty and righteousness" would establish an honourable peace that would bring about the "liberties, the freedom, and civilization of the human race." Mr Blocksidge went on to say how important it was to welcome home those who were returning from combat, and to build a better nation. "Is it not important that the church of Christ should take an active interest in these matters of employment, housing, social troubles, evils of disease, the danger and damage of strong drink etc.?" These were themes he was to return to in his 1921 and 1922 letters when he expressly referred to those "who are suffering from lack of employment, food or health" and "the distress and sorrow arising from the great industrial trials."

At the Deacons Meeting on 13th November 1918 it was announced that there would be a Thanksgiving Service held on 17th November. The Mayor had asked to be present along with the council, the officials, the police and the fire brigade.

Mr Blocksidge's New Year letter in 1918 also made passing reference to his own "illness and affliction" the previous year. In December 1918 the pastor was absent from the Church Meeting, and a letter was sent to Mr & Mrs Blocksidge "in their prolonged sickness." His 1919 New Year Letter said that "It is a matter of great regret and a cause of serious thought to me that my illness has been so prolonged." The nature of that illness is not specified, but he indicated that it "came in the cause of duty."

On 26th April 1922 the Church Meeting sent "hearty congratulations" to the pastor and Mrs Blocksidge on their Golden Wedding Anniversary. A double celebration was held in June that year to mark not only the Golden Wedding but also Mr Blocksidge's 41st Anniversary at the church. Incredibly, the event was attended by the Lord Bishop of Rochester, the Dean of Rochester, the Vicar of St Mark's, and a host of other clergy and civic leaders. The Bishop commended Mr Blocksidge on his role as a pastor, and stood in admiration for being able to preach to the same congregation for 41 years! The Dean also expressed his admiration for the Baptist minister's courtesy and politeness, and saw in Blocksidge's ecumenical spirit a model that all clergy should copy. Mr Dyke made presentations to the pastor on behalf of the congregation, and Mr Blocksidge replied that it was the most difficult moment he had ever experienced. He was quite overwhelmed by the kindness and generosity shown to him.

In February 1923 Mr Blocksidge, now aged 72, "made certain statements relating to his position as pastor and to the future." Nothing more was recorded and nothing further seems to have happened. On 24th March 1924 at the Church Meeting the pastor gave thanks to God for restoring him to health. He also gave thanks to the deacons for helping him throughout his recent illness. In May 1924 the pastor expressed a desire to retire at the end of the year. The deacons response to this was to draft in extra help with the pulpit supply and the visiting. No retirement came. In January 1925 Mrs Blocksidge died, and in May 1925 the pastor again informed the deacons of his intention of retiring at the end of the year "in consequence of the state of his health." This time the deacons did take him seriously.

The church was informed of his intention on Sunday 17th May. A Special Church Meeting was called for Monday 25th May at which the pastor's formal letter of resignation was read out. Mr Blocksidge expressed the opinion that the work needed a man in full vigour to lead the church forward. Farewell Services were planned for Sunday 29th November with a Public Meeting on 2nd December. Before that it was agreed that Mr Blocksidge should be granted the title 'Pastor Emeritus' (October 1925). At a Civic Ceremony held on 23rd September the town council conferred on Mr Blocksidge the title of Honorary Freeman of the Borough. The 'Gillingham Observer' in covering the Farewell Services made mention of the fact that during Blocksidge's tenure of office six young men had received calls to Christian Ministry and had gone to train at Spurgeon's College. Three of these, Revs T. Murray, F. Skinner and E. Tweed had already 'passed over the Great Divide' while Revs E. W. Mills, S. Tweed, and A. Hodge were serving churches at Torquay, Southsea and Hull.

The last Church Meeting Mr Blocksidge chaired was on 13th December 1925, although he did attend the meetings in January and March 1926 giving a brief address at the end of each.

1.   As well as heading up the local Band of Hope at Gillingham Baptist Church, Mr Blocksidge was also appointed to the Executive Committee of the Kent Band of Hope Union when it was formed in 1894

CHAPTER 4

A NEW ERA: MR REYNOLDS 1926 – 1936

Once Mr Blocksidge's decision to retire was taken seriously by the deacons they wasted no time in looking for his successor. By 1925 the Baptist Union was developing quite effective systems of denominational organisation. A Superannuation (pension) scheme, for example, was up and running, which Gillingham joined in 1927. And the settlement of ministers was being principally handled by a full time General Superintendent Minister in each of the twelve Areas.

On October 20th 1925 Rev Thomas Woodhouse, the General Superintendent for the Southern Area, met the deacons at Green Street. One of the first issues he raised with them was the need for a manse. He also mentioned issues such as an appropriate salary for any incoming minister. A package of £300 plus manse seemed about right, Mr Woodhouse told them. At that same meeting (and Mr Blocksidge hadn't had his leaving services yet) the deacons were presented with eight names of prospective ministers.

The method by which the church decided to choose its next minister would be frowned upon today. They decided to hold something of a preaching competition, and to invite three of the candidates over three successive Sundays. On March 8th 1926 a Special Church Meeting was held and the members were asked to vote for which of the three they preferred. The majority vote (196 out of 218) was for Rev F.V. Mildred. The meeting ended with Mr Blocksidge pronouncing himself perfectly satisfied with this decision. Rev Mildred, however, had other ideas and declined their invitation.

In June 1926 the church agreed to the purchase of a manse at 52 Linden Road. The property cost £625 and they financed this by taking out a £600 loan from the bank. They had looked at other properties but found them to be too expensive. One on Marlborough Road cost £850, while one on Balmoral Road was available for £1,150. Thanks were expressed to one of the deacons, Mr Woods, who had organised the purchase of the Linden Road property.

On 13th July 1926, following another preaching competition, a Church Meeting was held and a ballot taken as to which of three ministers the members preferred. This time the voting was much closer. Rev O. Allwright received 32 votes, Rev G.W. Bevan 54 votes, and Rev W.T. Reynolds 47 votes. When a second ballot was taken, removing the name of Mr Allwright, it transpired that Bevan received 67 votes and Reynolds 65. It was decided to invite both men back for a second preach.

On 17th August 1926 the Church Meeting voted again on the merits of the two men with Mr Bevan receiving 63 votes and Mr Reynolds 115. This was over the 60% threshold they had decided was necessary, and as a result an invitation to Mr Reynolds was issued. Reynolds did not take long to reply in the affirmative. At a Deacons Meeting held on 30th August Mr Dyke, the Church Secretary, read out a letter of acceptance from Mr Reynolds who was the minister at Bishops Stortford Baptist Church. The meeting was tinged with sadness, however, when Mr Dyke informed his colleagues that he would have to resign at the end of the year due to ill health. The meeting expressed sympathy "with our brother in his prolonged pain and illness."

The Church Meeting in October 1926, which read out Mr Reynolds' letter of acceptance, was also a very subdued occasion. Mr Woods, who chaired the meeting, had the painful duty of asking the meeting to stand in memory of their late Church Secretary, Mr Albert Dyke, who had recently passed away. A letter was sent to his widow, a copy of which was appended to the minutes. In the letter Mr Woods told her that "they desired to place on record the church's high appreciation of his sterling character and qualities, also his long, faithful and efficient work given unstintingly to the church at the Tabernacle, and which meant at all times a sacrifice of valuable time, at the cost of his general health."

Albert Dyke had taken on the role of Church Secretary following the death of Mr Nearn in 1899. But he had combined this roll with that of Church Treasurer following Mr Strugnell's departure for Southsea in 1912. In April 1919 there had been a suggestion of splitting the two jobs again, but Mr Dyke had taken exception to this, and the matter was shelved. In the church archives there is an illustrated Testimonial plaque to Mr Dyke dated 14th June 1926 which is signed by the pastor and deacons. It makes mention of the various offices he had held within the life of the church and concludes: "The deep interest in the church life, the self sacrifice you have made and the loyalty you have shown in your long record of work, have won our admiration, gained our heartfelt gratitude, and our highest praise." With the death of Mr Dyke it was decided that Mr John H. Ward would take on the role of Secretary while brother Winfield would serve as Treasurer.

Mr Reynolds chaired his first Deacons Meeting on 27th September, the day after he and his wife arrived in Gillingham! He chaired a Church Meeting on 8th November while his Recognition Services took place on 17th November. Speakers at the Recognition Services included Rev Thomas Woodhouse, the General Superintendent, and Mr Blocksidge!

William Thomas Reynolds was already an experienced Baptist Minister by the time he arrived in Gillingham. After training at Spurgeon's College he exercised a ten year ministry (1906 – 1916) at Wantage in Berkshire. This was followed by three years at Rickmansworth before moving to Bishops Stortford in 1920. By the time he started his ministry at Green Street, therefore, he already had twenty years of ministerial experience behind him.

In January 1927 it was agreed to hold Infant Dedication Services. A decision to move to individual communion cups was deferred until the April when a vote in favour of the move was agreed by 58 votes to 31. Brothers Fieldgate and Redcliffe offered to purchase the communion glasses to save the church any expense.

A bombshell came in February 1927, however, when Mr Reynolds informed the Church Meeting that the manse was wholly unsuitable. "It was not sufficiently commodious for the requirements of a pastor." The study never received any sunshine, and the manse was the smallest of all the Non-Conformist manses in the town. To have such a small manse, considered Mr Reynolds, was a poor reflection on the church!

The new Church Secretary, Mr J.H. Ward spoke in favour of selling the manse. He had already identified a property at 59 Rock Avenue which he believed was more suitable, and while the property cost £200 more than the current manse he believed that they could spread the additional cost over twenty years. A week later, at a follow up Church Meeting, the sale of Linden Road and the purchase of Rock Avenue were agreed. At the same time Mr Woods, who had handled the original purchase of 52 Linden Road, tendered his resignation from the diaconate and asked that his and his wife's names be removed from the Church Roll. The church struggled to know what to do with Mr Woods' resignation. Eventually events overtook the situation, and in September 1927 the deacons were informed that Mr Woods had passed away.

A second Church Meeting in February 1927 received a letter from the Baptist Church in Sutton, Surrey requesting the membership transfer of Rev W.W. Blocksidge who was now worshipping with them. The Pastor Emeritus had moved to live with his son and daughter-in-law in London. This was by no means the end of Mr Blocksidge's links with the church. During Mr Reynold's summer holidays from 1927 – 1932 Mr Blocksidge conducted services. He made regular appearances at reunions, Anniversaries, and Camden Road events. He also had a role in the Jubilee (50 years) celebrations of the Tab. in 1929 at which again the Mayor and Corporation were in attendance.

In September 1930, to mark Mr Blocksidge's 80th birthday, a social evening was held down at the church. He was presented with a portrait of himself, the work of Messrs Howe of Chatham, and a drawing of the Tab.. He was allowed to keep the drawing, but handed the portrait back to be displayed in the schoolroom. In speeches that were made, Mr H.T. Sanders referred to Mr Blocksidge as the Grand Old Man of the Baptist denomination, "at any rate as far as Kent was concerned." Warm praise was also given by Mr Reynolds. In responding to their kind words Mr Blocksidge concluded by speaking in "appreciative terms of his successor" and expressed the hope that Mr Reynolds would have "a long, happy and useful association with the Tabernacle."

In late 1927 it was decided to purchase the new Baptist Church Hymnal for worship at the Tab.. The congregation were asked if they would like to buy their own copies. In 1928 a branch of the Baptist Women's League was formed. And in 1929 a Junior Church Membership was formed for those aged 11-16 who were active workers in the Christian Endeavour or Band of

Hope. In 1928 a proposal by Mr Raymond Tranah, to abolish the pew rents and have all free sittings instead, was rejected by the deacons as unworkable.

At the end of the AGM in January 1930 Mr Sanders, one of the senior deacons, "spoke in a very appreciative way of the services of our pastor, and of the esteem in which he is held." He went on to commend the pastor for "his sound doctrine, and the preaching of the word" as a consequence of which he "had drawn the hearts of the members to him." He concluded by referring to "the much appreciated service and activities of Mrs W. T. Reynolds and the useful work in which she was engaged." Thanks were expressed to them both, and the commendation was carried unanimously.

Perhaps the major event in Mr Reynold's ministry at Green Street was the construction of The Institute. In May 1931 Mr Rowland Tranah proposed that steps should be taken towards the provision of a Young Men's Institute building. A committee was formed to draw up proposals. They reported back to the June Church Meeting and presented two options from a builder. The second option was preferred which involved constructing a single storey 42 foot long brick building on the site occupied by the two gardens of the cottages. It would also require demolishing parts of the cottages themselves, although some of the rooms could be utilised for other purposes. The Church Meeting agreed the plans and the tenants were asked to vacate the two cottages.

By October 1931 one of the tenants had vacated but the other remained. By March 1932 this tenant was still in residence and was holding up the whole project. The church decided to take drastic action, and in May 1932 they purchased a property at 171 Victoria Street for £290 with the sole aim of moving the Green Street tenant in there.

1932 marked a couple of celebrations. Mr and Mrs Reynolds celebrated their silver wedding anniversary, and Mr Hyde Nicholson completed thirty years as the church organist. The Tab. also hosted the Kent and Sussex Baptist Association in 1932.

The Institute building was completed in early 1933. Issues arose early on such as whether card games were permitted. The Church Meeting (April 1933) decided they were not to be allowed.

The work at Camden Road was also developing well. The annual reports for the Mission are available from 1931 and give a helpful snapshot of its progress. The report for 1932 - 33, for example, said that there were 310 scholars on the Sunday School Roll with 30 Teachers. There were also 30 guides, 24 cubs, 25 scouts as well as 11 rovers! The Band of Hope was reported as thriving as was the Women's Meeting and the Evening Mission. The Report for 1933 - 1934 said that the Evening Mission attendances were on average between 30 and 40 but Parade Services could be as high as 70 to 80. The Report for 1936 - 37 said that there were 105 names on the Band of Hope register while average attendance at the Tuesday evening meeting was 80. The number of Sunday School scholars had dropped to 194.

One of the innovations during Mr Reynolds' ministry was the introduction of the 'Tabernacle Tidings'. This was a monthly magazine which began in March 1927. It contained an article by the minister, and then 'Church Notes' by Mr Ward, the Church Secretary, along with other items of news from the Sunday School, the Choir, the Ladies Sewing Circle, Christian Endeavour, Band of Hope, and Camden Road. Every month there was also a long article about the work of the Baptist Missionary Society. The 'Tidings' was originally funded entirely by local adverts which often ran to several pages. Shopkeepers along the length of the High Street feature in the magazine including Mr Hyde Nicholson's funeral business, and Mr Fieldgate's shop which specialised in oysters.

The 'Tabernacle Tidings' provides lots of information not picked up by the Deacons or Church Meeting minutes. In March 1927, for example, Mr Follett was presented with a bound copy of the Schofield Reference Bible for thirty years' service as Secretary and Superintendent of the Sunday School. In June 1929 Mr Reynolds went as part of a British Free Church fact finding tour of Canada visiting Montreal, Quebec and Toronto. In 1932 he was part of a group visiting Germany, and was able to observe first-hand the destitution and suffering the German people were experiencing. In 1935 he visited Scandinavia, and sampled church life in Norway, Sweden and Denmark.

Mr Reynolds used his monthly column in the 'Tidings' to address some of his personal concerns. A couple of times he bemoaned the threat to The Lord's Day posed by the campaign to open cinemas on Sundays. He wrote of the need for a religious revival in the country; the need for Christians to exercise their democratic responsibilities; and in March 1935 he wrote passionately about the German government's wickedness in persecuting the Jews.

One of the most enlightening articles that Mr Reynolds penned was in June 1933. He had been very unwell, and wrote in part to thank everyone for their kind thoughts and good wishes during his illness. But he also took the opportunity to reflect on the life of a Baptist Minister in the 1930s:

"For six years I have regularly preached five times every week, visited a minimum of 20 hospital wards weekly, and done the pastoral work of a large church besides rendering constant help to other churches and societies. It is all a constant joy, and is infinitely worthwhile, but body and brain do grow weary sometimes. I have a parish of 54 miles of streets, and one bicycle to get round it. Calls are constant. During the last two weeks before I went sick I was called out of bed six times in the early hours of the morning to minister to the dying, and in every case I was glad to have had the opportunity."

Mr Reynolds ended his article by saying that he had just purchased a car, and dedicated it to God's service.

The 'Tidings' also gave the Church Secretary opportunities to vent issues that were of concern to him. In September 1929, for example, Mr Ward remarked that "Many of our friends are noted for being just too late for the commencement of the worship of God." Why not try to arrive five minutes early?!! In November 1932 Mr Ward mentioned the sixth Anniversary of Mr Reynolds' ministry at the Tab.. He expressed thanks to God for "sending to us such a worthy successor to the Gospel ministry of our late pastor, Rev W.W. Blocksidge." And in the summer of 1936 Mr Ward referred to an offer of a plot of land on the Darland estate as a location for another Baptist Church. Mr A. E. Clifford, who made the offer, was thanked for his generosity which the church would strive to act upon "when the time is ripe for such a venture." (Oct.1936). Events were to conspire in such a way that this opportunity was never taken up.

As early as 1934 there seemed to be a certain malaise in the life of the church. The Camden Road Mission was struggling, and Mr Jewell presented a bleak assessment of the situation at the March Deacons Meeting. There was too much to do and not enough workers. The Church Meeting in April 1934 caused the pastor some consternation when brother John Smith stated that there was an apathy in the church that needed addressing. Mr Reynolds took the comment personally. And in July the Church Meeting was informed that a majority of the deacons had asked the pastor to relinquish his position as chaplain of the Medway Infirmary and to concentrate on his work at the Tab.. A vote of confidence was called for which Mr Reynolds won "with no dissension". Nevertheless this must have been a very difficult period. The Church Meeting in November 1935 spent a considerable amount of time in heartfelt prayer for the success of the work and ministry of the church. The Annual Meeting in January 1936 reported a financial deficit of nearly £60 in the year.

The financial anxieties and lack of ambition meant that bold initiatives were not being pursued. An attempt to bring in a full time worker for Camden Road from the Spurgeon's Colporteur Association was turned down (October 1934). And Mr Clifford's renewed attempt to get the church to start a new work on Darland (September 1936) seemed to receive the same response.

Matters came to a crisis in the Church Meeting of September 1936 when the Brotherhood asked if they could have lady speakers at their meetings. "The pastor stated that it was his supreme conviction that a woman should not speak to a mixed assembly in the Tab.." There was a prolonged discussion which must have got out of hand because two of the deacons proposed that the meeting be closed. This was by no means the end of the matter. The Brotherhood decided to pre-empt matters by passing their own resolution (September 23rd) in favour of having lady speakers. Mr Reynolds saw this as undermining his authority and tendered his resignation (October 3rd). The Deacons (October 5th) accepted the pastor's resignation, but when this was referred to the Church Meeting on the 12th October (Rev Sutton, the Area Superintendent in the chair) a sizeable minority (62 votes to 82) wanted Mr Reynolds to reconsider his resignation. In the end the meeting agreed to ask Mr Reynolds to stay with them until the following September. He declined and insisted that he would conclude his ministry at the end of the year.

Correspondence during October between Mr Sutton, the Area Superintendent, and Mr Ward makes clear the very real danger that the church could split over the matter. The General Secretary of the Baptist Union, Rev M. E. Aubrey, was drawn into the controversy, at one point (November 24th) having to scotch a rumour that Mr Ward had asked for Mr Reynolds to be removed from the list of accredited Baptist Ministers. Eventually Mr Reynolds concluded his ministry at the Tab. at the end of December, and the 'Rochester and Gillingham News' carried a very civilized account of his Farewell. Speeches were made and presentations given. There was appreciation of his ten years of ministry and the faithful pastoral work carried out by the minister.

In the New Year the press continued to follow Mr Reynolds' movements. Mr Reynolds had objected strongly to an article in the 'Chatham Observer' in the autumn of 1936 to the effect that he was looking to take on a church from another denomination. But in January 1937 the 'Chatham Observer' was able to announce that William Thomas Reynolds had been ordained by the Bishop of Rochester as curate of All Saints Parish Church, Belvedere on March 14th 1937. Mr Reynolds continued to exercise ministry in the Church of England, serving parishes in Tunbridge Wells, Bexleyheath (Barnehurst), Upper Norwood, and finally, in 1951, as chaplain to Bromley College. A note in the Church Members Roll indicates that Mr Reynolds died on February 14th 1966, aged 85.

With Mr Reynolds' hasty departure there was a huge vacuum to fill. Who better to fill the vacuum than Rev W. W. Blocksidge! The Church Meeting in January 1937 (again chaired by Rev Sutton, the Area Superintendent) reported a request from Mr Blocksidge to have his membership transferred from Sutton, Surrey to Gillingham. The meeting was delighted. The February 'Tidings' informed the readers that Mr Blocksidge would act as

Authorized Person for weddings during the vacancy, and he subsequently conducted one wedding on 31ˢᵗ March. The March 'Tidings' printed Mr Blocksidge's name as the Pastor Emeritus. He was residing at 2 Barnsole Road, Gillingham. Mr Blocksidge and four others were received into membership on March 4ᵗʰ, and he led in prayer at the April Church Meeting following the death of some older church members.

Blocksidge was by this time 86 years old. Mr Ward, in the 'Tidings' for November 1935, commented that Mr Blocksidge, who had conducted services for them the previous month, "seems to have learned the secret of perpetual youth". By the following June, however, the Church Secretary had reported that Mr Blocksidge had undergone a serious operation, albeit making a full recovery.

His arrival in Gillingham was to be short lived. On 12ᵗʰ April he was present for the Church's 58ᵗʰ Anniversary, but on 22ⁿᵈ April he was taken ill, and he died of pneumonia on 23ʳᵈ April. On Sunday 25ᵗʰ April Mr Ward was away in Manchester so that the task of giving out the notices fell to Mr Winfield. The church archive still contains his hand written notes for that day. After announcing the various things that were happening that week Mr Winfield went on to say:

"It now falls to my lot to announce that our very dear friend and pastor – the Rev W. W. Blocksidge passed away in the early hours of Friday last." Mr Winfield provided details of the funeral arrangements and the memorial service and concluded, one imagines fighting back the tears, "He who stood on this spot for so many years and led us in our worship is no longer with us. No more may we hear his voice or clasp his hand but we give thanks to God for every remembrance of him."

Mr Blocksidge's funeral took place on Tuesday 27ᵗʰ April, 58 years to the day since the formation of the church. The service was conducted by Rev W. Lomax Mackenzie of Broadstairs. Blocksidge was 'laid in state' in the church for people to pay their respects before being buried in the Grange Road Cemetery alongside his late wife. Flags were lowered to half-mast on all public buildings. On the following Sunday, May 2ⁿᵈ 1937, a Memorial Service was held for him conducted by Revs S. G. Tweed and B. G.

Nicholson. They had been Sunday School scholars and members of the Tab. during Mr Blocksidge's ministry.

Mr Winfield, the Church Treasurer, had grown up during Mr Blocksidge's ministry. He recalled as a very young boy having Blocksidge kneel and pray with him following his father's death. It was the start of Winfield's long association with the church. Now, in the May edition of 'The Tidings', he gave his 'appreciation' of the great man's achievements. He retraced the key events of Mr Blocksidge's ministry; described the honours that had been bestowed upon him; and finally he ended with words from John Oxenham:

"Great heart is dead they say – what is death to such a one as Great Heart?' ..... He lives on. His name shall kindle many a heart to equal flame. The flame he lighted shall burn on and on. *A soul so sweet can never die, but lives and loves and works through all eternity."*

In September 1950 Mr Winfield organised a celebration of Mr Blocksidge's ministry to coincide with what would have been Blocksidge's 100th birthday.

CHAPTER 5

THE SECOND WORLD WAR: MR SOAR AND MR BARNARD

The slide during the 1930s was all too plain. The vestry report in January 1937 recorded a membership total of 369 plus 14 permanent communicant members. But the March Deacons Meeting brought forward 64 names for deletion! The offerings for the year, which had totalled £628 in 1928, had dropped year on year until in 1937 they were only £546. The task for whoever took over the pastorate was not an easy one.

In April 1937 the favoured candidate for the vacant pastorate was 27 year old Mr Claude William Lapsley from Spurgeon's College. He preached twice that month and the Church Meeting on 19th April voted 143 to 5 to invite him to the church. He had already indicated that the manse was unsuitable, but the church were willing to do something about that. Remarkably, Mr Lapsley turned them down. One of his letters to Mr Ward indicated dissatisfaction with the level of salary being offered. According to the June edition of the 'Tidings' he accepted a call to High Road, Tottenham.

The second serious candidate for the pastorate was Mr Cecil Josiah Soar. Remarkably, people still remembered his visit to them as a student from Spurgeon's College back in 1927. Mr Soar was pastor of City Road Baptist Church, Birmingham, and prior to that he had served for three years as minister at Burnham-on-Crouch in Essex. He had also served in the Royal Navy during the First World War. The Church Meeting on 12th September 1937 voted 112 to 10 to invite him to the pastorate with 6 abstentions. Throughout the rest of September discussions went on between Mr Soar and the deacons regarding the suitability or otherwise of the manse. Finally on 2nd October Mr Soar telegrammed Mr Ward to accept the pastorate. He commenced his ministry in January 1938 with Recognition Services taking place on 26th January. The day was somewhat overtaken by the fact that the church chose that occasion to unveil the Memorial Tablet to Mr Blocksidge which members of the congregation had paid for over the previous months.

During 1938 Mr Jewell expressed his desire to step down from the Superintendency of Camden Road Mission. He continued to exercise a role at the Mission but was to relinquish overall control.

The work at the Tab. continued and picked up. There were baptisms, and there was an increase in the weekly offerings. But the back drop to everything that was happening in the church was the deteriorating international situation. Writing in the 'Tidings' in October 1938, Mr Soar put down his own feelings:

"We are all anxious that peace may yet be saved, especially those of us who know the bitter experience of war....... There is nothing glamorous or heroic or fine in the bloodshed, the heartbreak, the bestiality, the mad ruin of war. Let us resort more and more to God in earnest prayer that He will yet spare us the unspeakable calamity of war, and preserve us the blessing of peace."

In December 1938 Mr Ward expressed his thanks to Mr Soar on completing his first year as their pastor, a year of "steady progress."

The beginning of 1939 was taken over by elaborate preparations for the Diamond Jubilee celebrations of the church. Four days of events were planned between 26th and 29th March. Speakers over the four days included Rev Frederick James Humphrey, the Baptist Union President; Dr John Charles Carlile, the editor of the Baptist Times; Sir Robert Gower MP; and Rt. Hon Ernest Brown, the Minister of Labour. The Re-Union Supper on the Tuesday night saw 300 people in the schoolroom and adjacent classrooms. The final meeting on Wednesday night ended with the choir singing the 'Hallelujah Chorus'. As a tangible expression of the celebrations Mr Soar conceived the idea of starting a Diamond Jubilee Fund with a target of £500 for future work at the church. Promises made over the four day period yielded £364, but it was not until March 1942 that the target was finally achieved.

The proceedings of the Diamond Jubilee celebrations were followed minutely by both the 'Kent Observer' (1st April 1939) and the 'Chatham, Rochester and Gillingham News' (31st March 1939). Verbatim accounts of Dr Carlile's address and that of Rt. Hon Ernest Brown were provided.

There was an overwhelming belief that the health of the town was related to the health of the church. The Mayoress said that the town of Gillingham had grown up around the Tab. and she referred to the Tab. as the "foundation stone" of Gillingham. Other contributors spoke of the wonderful influence the Tab. had exercised on the thousands of children and young people who had passed through its doors.

In April 1939 Mr Soar asked permission of the deacons to submit his name as a chaplain to the armed forces in the event of war breaking out. The deacons agreed to this suggestion, stating that they would keep his post at Green Street open for him, should the need arise, while he was away on duty. In June 1939 a telephone was installed at the manse.

In July Mr Ward, the Church Secretary, took the decision to leave the district. He and his wife decided to move to Portsmouth. So suddenly was their departure that the church did not have the opportunity to say a proper farewell. In the end the church turned to Mr Winfield to take on the role of Church Secretary in addition to his existing role as Church Treasurer.

In September war was officially declared against Germany. There was a frenzy of activity, and one of the first noticeable effects was the decimation of the Sunday School caused by evacuation. Numbers of children in the towns dropped appreciably. With many of the men in church working at the dockyard on Sundays there was a marked drop in numbers attending the morning service. Blackout materials for the church windows had to be made, and for a time the Tab. moved its evening service to the afternoon, although this was not a popular move.

At a Deacons Meeting on the afternoon of 8th October Mr Soar informed his colleagues that he had received his call-up. In fact he was able to remain in the district for several more months providing pulpit supply but being unavailable for pastoral duties during the week. In January 1940 it was mutually agreed that as a result of these changes Mr Soar's wages would be reduced to £2. 10 shillings per week. The photograph of Mr Soar which appeared on the front of the 'Tidings' was changed in the January edition. Instead of sporting his clerical attire he now appeared in army uniform.

With the impending departure of the pastor, and his lack of availability to carry out pastoral duties, the deacons turned their minds to finding a substitute. The idea that received most support among the deacons was of joining forces with Rochester Baptist Church. Rev Walter Albert Butcher from Rochester was no stranger to the Green Street congregation. He had made several visits over the years and was widely appreciated. The suggestion was that he would conduct alternate morning and evening services at the two churches, and be available to do urgent pastoral visits. In the end this scheme collapsed when, in April 1940, Rev Butcher accepted a call to become pastor of Frinton-on-Sea Baptist Church.

The early part of 1940 was taken up with issues surrounding the trusteeship of the church. Since its inception Gillingham Baptist Church had operated with private trustees who were the legal guardians of the charity. These were separate to the deacons although there was often overlap. Major decisions on buildings and money always needed to be referred to the trustees. In February 1940 it was reported that the Trust Deed specified that there should be nine trustees. In fact they were now down to five and three of these wished to resign. At a Deacons Meeting in March 1940, chaired by Rev Soar, a letter was read out from Rev M. E. Aubrey, General Secretary of the Baptist Union, suggesting that the Baptist Union could act as trustees of the church. This seemed to attract some interest, and at the June Deacons meeting it was recorded that Rev Aubrey was drawing up the necessary paperwork. The process was never completed, however, because by the end of the year the church solicitor was drawing up a memorandum to add seven new names to the surviving trustees. The short-sightedness of this move was brought home in December 1940 when one of those to be made a trustee, Mr Bernard V. Tranah, was killed in an air raid at Chatham Dockyard. This was a major blow to the church because Mr Tranah was Sunday School Superintendent and also one of the deacons. Mr Bennett, who was also included in the new list of trustees, died in April 1941.

The war was already taking its toll on the church. Two more fatalities were recorded in 1940: Mr F. Drake was killed on active service, while Mrs Walters died of injuries received during an air raid. In the July edition of the 'Tidings' Mr Winfield reported that twenty members of the Tab.

community were on active service. Many others were engaged in work connected with the war.

In the August 'Tidings' the Sunday School notes commented: "So many scholars have been evacuated once more that our numbers are reduced to a mere skeleton of what they used to be." In the October 1940 edition Mr Winfield provided a stark assessment of the effect that the constant air raids and air raid sirens were having on church life: "Some of our services have been disturbed, others have been abandoned, and what is more, quite a number of our people have suffered almost irreparable disaster in the loss of their homes." Twelve families from the church had been affected this way. In September 1940 Mr Soar, absent from Medway since August, wrote to the deacons offering the use of the manse to Mr Bagnall and his family who had been rendered homeless through an air raid. The deacons agreed, and the Bagnalls gratefully moved into 59 Rock Avenue.

The Sunday School notes for the December edition of the 'Tidings' reported that for some weeks the Sunday School had not been able to meet because of air raid warnings and parents being unwilling to let their children go out. Numbers of children attending Sunday School were reduced to an average of six in the morning and twelve in the afternoon.

Mr Soar continued to keep in contact with the church while he was away on duty. He was never able to disclose his location but it appeared that he remained in Britain ministering to soldiers who were in training. Each month he supplied a letter for the 'Tidings'. In January 1941 he told the people back in Gillingham: "My work now is so different from what it was when I am with you. One doesn't preach sermons to soldiers. They are just five or ten minute talks." He did make occasional visits back to Green Street. He was back in his pulpit on December 22nd 1940 and again on August 3rd 1941. The previous evening he had been present at a Deacons Meeting. But for the most part the church was relying on pulpit supply week by week. Once again Spurgeon's College provided invaluable support. In the summer of 1940 various students from Spurgeon's took services including Mr Charles Jack Pike. In January 1941 there was a satisfactory report of the visit of another Spurgeon's student, Mr George Beasley-Murray. One of the church's own members, Mr Louis Read, took services during this period. Unusually he was training for the ministry at Regents Park College.

Following the failure to secure the services of Mr Butcher as temporary pastor, the deacons spent several months considering other possible candidates, but none of these came to anything. In July 1941 the Church Secretary, Mr Winfield, told the deacons of his intention to write to Mr Soar asking him to resign his chaplaincy and return full time to Green Street. When Mr Soar met the deacons in August he agreed that he would look into the possibility of returning to civilian life. This clearly never materialised because at a Church Meeting on Saturday 29th November 1941 a formal proposal was put to the meeting from the deacons asking them to urge Mr Soar to resign his chaplaincy and return to his pastorate at Green Street. When the proposition was put to the meeting, however, there were only 21 votes in support of the deacons' suggestion, and 26 against. Instead, on brother Crawford's proposition, the Church Meeting resolved to assure the pastor of their full support. The deacons were asked to pursue the search for a temporary pastor.

Saturday 14th February 1942 was the Church Annual Meeting. Mr Soar was present and took the chair. The death was recorded of Mr F. Huxstep who had been a deacon for 29 years. The vestry report informed the members that there were now 314 members on Roll with 16 further communicants. Offerings for 1941 totalled just over £511. The meeting also mentioned that a student from Spurgeon's College, Mr Reginald Barnard, had recently taken services to good effect. Could we have him again? Mr Winfield had also mentioned Mr Barnard's preaching in a 'Tidings' article in November 1941. He was an Australian, and came "with a style that was somewhat new to us" and with a directness that was unusual. Nevertheless he clearly appealed to members, and at a Church Meeting on 18th March 1942 Mr Barnard was offered the temporary pastorate "without any dissent". In answer to the question, 'how long will this be for?' the answer recorded in the minutes was "until Mr Soar is able to resume his ministry." Mr Barnard accepted the position in the April, and the May 'Tidings' recorded Mr Soar's delight at the arrangement. He wished the 27 year old young man every success. Mr Barnard's Recognition Services were fixed for Wednesday 29th July and Mr Soar was present to carry out the act of Induction. The July edition of the 'Tidings' carried the names of both ministers on the front page, and there were articles from both men in the issue. Mr Barnard told his readers that he had never intended to remain in Britain after training but had assumed he would return to Australia. Obviously God had other plans.

One of the immediate problems the church had to address was accommodation for Mr Barnard. The manse, which would have been the obvious place, was already occupied by the Bagnall family. A suggestion at the May Deacons Meeting was whether Mr Barnard, a single man, could lodge with the Bagnalls. In the end it was decided to rent a property further down from the manse at 51 Rock Avenue, and Mr Barnard moved in there during the summer of 1942. He chaired his first Deacons Meeting on August 7th and his first Church Meeting on August 17th. The most immediate and pressing problem to face was Camden Road.

The September edition of the 'Tidings' referred to the fact that Mr Richard Jewell was stepping down as Superintendent of the Mission after 15 years. Mr Winfield's own assessment of the situation raised doubts as to the continued viability of the Mission. There was a need to consider its future. Sometimes the Holy Spirit prompts us forward, but sometimes he urges restraint. Not put off by this potential crisis, Mr Barnard followed up a possibility which had been considered but rejected in Mr Reynolds' time: The Spurgeon's Colporteur Association. This was an evangelistic organisation which trained lay pastors for mission projects just like Camden Road. The cost to the church of the scheme was estimated at £105 for the year. At other times this might have proved too daunting, but desperate times required desperate measures and the deacons gave the green light to pursue possible candidates. Two factors that would have helped the calculation was firstly that the mortgage on the manse had been paid off in November 1942, and secondly the Diamond Jubilee Fund was inching ever closer to its £500 target. Throughout the latter half of 1942 names of potential colporteurs were considered but nothing came of them. Finally in February 1943 the name of Thomas Gilbert Lloyd emerged. He proved very acceptable, and in the March an invitation was extended to him to take charge at Camden Road for a period of twelve months. Mr Lloyd accepted. He and his wife, Blodwen, had their membership transferred from Eythorne Baptist Church, Dover, and they formally took up their post in September 1943. The October edition of the 'Tidings' had

Mr Lloyd recorded as 'pastor' of Camden Road. He and his wife were living at 317 Woodlands Road, Gillingham.

Having taken this major initiative, Mr Barnard now had pressing matters of his own to deal with. At the Deacons Meeting in February 1943 he informed those present of his intention of getting married in June. His bride to be was Mary Denly from Redhill Tabernacle. Congratulations were naturally offered, but the pressing issue was where the couple were to live. The manse was the obvious option. This was now a real possibility because the Bagnalls had found another property and were in the process of moving out. But what was to be done with Mr Soar's furniture?

The whole subject clearly became heated and complicated. Mr Soar was not happy, and neither was Mr Barnard. On April 10th the deacons had a meeting with Rev Sutton, the Area Superintendent, to try and find a way through the impasse. It clearly didn't work because the Church Meeting minute book contains a letter from Mr Barnard, dated 27th April 1943, in which he tendered his resignation. He said that he needed a permanent pastorate for his wife-to-be. The deacons saw no way forward but to accept his resignation, but when it was taken to the Church Meeting in May an amendment from the floor of the meeting was passed, namely that Mr Barnard be asked to defer his decision. The same meeting agreed to ask Mr Soar to move his furniture from the manse, and at the same time they decided to increase Mr Barnard's salary to £300 a year.

The Church Meeting on 1st June was informed that Mr Barnard had withdrawn his resignation. He had met with Mr Soar and the two of them had agreed that Mr Soar's furniture could be moved into two rooms of the manse while the Barnards used the rest. The Meeting made it clear, however, that they did not want this arrangement to last more than six months and that Mr Soar would need to find alternative storage for his belongings. Mr Barnard's contract was also clarified, extending it until the end of hostilities after which three months notice on either side.

May and June 1943 mark a change in the relationship between the church and Mr Soar. The 'Tidings' had carried articles by the two ministers alternately since August 1942. But May 1943 was the last edition to carry a lead article from Mr Soar. Every edition from that point onwards carried

Mr Barnard's comments and thoughts. A decision was also taken to defer the Church Anniversary which Mr Soar was due to take on 19th May. Mr Soar did represent the church, however, at Louis Read's Induction as minister of Nailsworth Baptist Church, Gloucestershire. Mr Soar gave the charge to the church and provided extracts from the day for the 'Tidings' in March 1944.

By this time events had taken a further twist. The deacons, at their meeting on 15th February 1944, were informed that Mr Barnard had decided that he ought to resign anyway. He explained to the church in March that he still felt something of a shadow hanging over him because of the 'temporary' status he occupied, and for the sake of his wife and parents, who had now come to settle in the UK, he needed to find a permanent position. The Barnards were to settle at Wellington Square Baptist Church, Hastings, and their Farewell at Green Street was on 5th November. Mr Barnard's last service was a baptismal service. After four years at Hastings the Barnard family took up ministry in Australia before returning to England and taking up pastorates in Hinckley, Leicestershire in 1954 and Abbey Road, St John's Wood, in 1959.

As soon as the deacons knew of Mr Barnard's resignation they wrote to Mr Soar informing him of the development and explaining that they did not wish to continue with a further temporary arrangement. This was in the February. At the Church Meeting on 4th March the deacons' position hardened. They recommended to the church that they set in motion plans to look for a settled pastor straightaway. Not everyone was happy with this, and an amendment was put from the floor of the meeting that Mr Soar be acquainted with developments and be asked to return. The amendment only received 13 votes and was consequently lost.

In April the deacons received a letter from Mr Soar reminding them of the freedom they gave him back in 1939 to leave for military service in the confidence that there would be a job available for him at the end. The deacons suggested meeting to discuss this in May at the Baptist Assembly in London. Mr Soar wrote back to say that he would not be attending the Assembly but that if they wished to travel over to Barry, in South Wales, to meet with him then he would be happy to discuss matters further. The deacons declined to make the journey. Instead on Saturday 13th May 1944 the deacons brought a recommendation to the Church Meeting that the decision of October 9th 1939 to allow Mr Soar to serve as chaplain be rescinded. The meeting agreed this by 57 votes to 23. A second proposition, that Mr Soar be asked to terminate his pastorate, received 50 votes to 26 which was a majority but not a two thirds majority to make it binding.

In June Mr Soar reluctantly gave the church permission to look for another minister, but attached several conditions which the deacons were not happy about. Consequently, on 26th July, a Church Meeting chaired by the Area Superintendent, Rev Sutton, was asked to consider the proposition "that the pastorate of Rev Cecil J Soar be terminated on 31st August 1944." The proposition was considered, agonised over, and eventually passed 80 votes to 27. It was also made clear that no intimation of these developments should be made known to the press.

Not everyone was happy with this decision. Several letters of complaint were received, and one of the deacons, Mr D. Bennett, resigned in protest at the treatment of the minister. His resignation was accepted with regret.

Mr Soar did not endear himself to the church by writing a letter to the Chatham News complaining of his treatment by the church. The letter appeared on the 8th September 1944. In it he explained to the public that he had not resigned but had been dismissed for reasons that he could not understand. The church had reneged on the agreement made with him at the outbreak of the war. Mr Soar thanked all those who had supported his ministry over the years, and went on to say, "My memory of Gillingham Tabernacle will be of a church with boundless possibilities but a narrow horizon: a grand crowd of youth, and an absence of good leadership." Not surprisingly the deacons were outraged that Mr Soar had published such statements in a local newspaper. Mr Winfield in his own diary entry for this period was incensed and documented the painstaking steps the church leaders had taken to resolve the predicament. The deacons sent copies of the letter to both Rev Sutton, the Area Superintendent, and to Rev M.E. Aubrey, the General Secretary of the Baptist Union. Both men deplored Rev Soar's actions but urged the deacons NOT to reply. The October edition of the 'Tidings' carried a brief note to the effect that anyone wishing to contribute towards a leaving gift for Rev and Mrs Soar should speak with either Rowland or Alan Tranah.

The search for a new, permanent, minister started in earnest in the autumn of 1944. Rev Sutton chaired Church Meetings in the October and the November. The November meeting voted NOT to accept Rev Joseph Tweedley as their minister. In February 1945 Rev Charles Jack Francis Pike, minister of the churches at Wendover and Aylesbury, had conducted services and had gone down well. He was invited to preach 'with a view' on 25th March. The subsequent Church Meeting on 4th April voted unanimously (73 votes to 0) to invite Rev Pike to the pastorate. Mr Pike accepted the invitation at a salary of £300 a year. He was to commence on 2nd September.

Mr Soar, meanwhile, was asked to remove his furniture from the manse by the end of July. The Church Meeting in June was informed that Mr Soar was refusing to do this whereupon it was decided that the only course of action available was to move his furniture into a couple of rooms down at the Tab.. Nothing is recorded as to whether this action was taken. There is simply a note in the Church Meeting minutes for October 1945 to say that "the matter of Rev Soar's furniture has been satisfactorily arranged."

There is a very sad footnote to all of this. The Church Membership Roll indicates that Mr and Mrs Soar transferred their membership to Harborne Baptist Church, Birmingham in July 1946. It also indicates that Mr Soar died on 16th February 1951. He was only 54 years old. The Harborne Baptist Church newsletter for March 1951 provided details of the funeral service at which both the Bishop and Archdeacon of Birmingham were in attendance. The Rev A.J. Klaiber, General Superintendent of the West Midlands Baptist Association, conducted the service which took place on Wednesday 21st February. About 200 people were in attendance. Numerous tributes were paid to the memory of Mr Soar who had served for nearly five years as minister of the church. One speaker said of him: "His was a gentle nature; he was always kind and considerate, yet he was capable of firmness in support of what he believed." The editor of the newsletter brought his own tribute, referring again to Mr Soar's gentle nature: "He has led but never driven, and has persuaded hearts and minds by his example." Mr Soar's obituary in the Baptist Handbook for 1952 indicated that he served as General Secretary of the West Midland Baptist Association from 1948. He left a widow, Florence, "and a young daughter to mourn his loss." The Harborne Baptist Church newsletter gave the name of his daughter as Valerie.

CHAPTER 6

POST – WAR RECONSTRUCTION: C.J. PIKE

Charles Jack Francis Pike (Jack) was born in 1914 in Newbury, Berkshire. He was a son of the manse and was brought up with his two brothers and two sisters. He was baptised by his father in the North East of England and trained at Spurgeon's College.

Mr Pike's acceptance of the call to the Gillingham pastorate coincided with the end of the Second World War. Mr Winfield's article in the 'Tidings' for June expressed jubilation at the ringing of church bells and the cessation of fighting in Europe. Mr Pike was to be a peace time minister. It wasn't until Remembrance Sunday 1949 that a Memorial was put in place to the eleven men and women from the church who had been killed in the Second World War. The Memorial was in the form of an oak Communion Table which was dedicated as part of that special service. It contained a plaque with the names of those who had given their lives between 1939 and 1945.

The October 'Tidings' gave a formal welcome to the new minister, and the report from the Green Street branch of the Baptist Women's League mentioned the welcome it had given to Mrs Marjorie Pike, their new President, and to Miss Daphne Pike as well. Mrs Pike was quickly into the role of minister's wife helping to organise the Harvest arrangements, and starting a crèche on a Sunday morning to allow young mothers to attend the morning service.

Mr Pike's first challenge, like his predecessor Mr Barnard, was the Camden Road Mission. Mr Lloyd, the Spurgeon's colporteur/pastor had done a tremendous job at the Mission. New organisations were started. There were several baptisms, an air of purpose, and in August 1944 he had been given permission to open a Building Fund for a new church building at Camden Road. The twelve month contract he was originally given was readily renewed. An indication of the progress the Mission was making can be found in the 'Tidings' for June 1945 which provided excerpts from the Mission Secretary's Annual Report produced the previous month:

"For two years the Mission has been under the leadership of Mr Lloyd. Many of our activities have been started since he came and are carried on under his personal supervision. We thank him for all he is doing and thank God for the progress that has been made. We give thanks too for the gracious ministry of Mrs Lloyd, even in the midst of suffering." The Report went on to list some of the groups and their relative strength that were operating under the Mission. The Sunday School had 102 scholars; the Girls Life Brigade had 41 members; the Boys Fellowship had 14 on the books while the Women's Meeting had 20. There was also the Christian Endeavour and the evening service to round off the work of Camden Road at that time. As the Mission celebrated its Silver Jubilee in 1946 it had probably never been in better heart or in better shape.

Alas, the bubble was shortly to burst. A Deacons Meeting in June 1946 heard from Rev Pike that Mr Lloyd had handed in his resignation with immediate effect following "certain moral failures." No specific information was provided, but in the July edition of the 'Tidings' Mr Pike was at pains to point out that no-one else from the Tab. or the Mission was involved. The church showed considerable anxiety for the welfare of Mrs Lloyd who had spent the previous 15 months at the Royal Sea Bathing Hospital in Margate.

In July the deacons considered various options for running the Mission. In the end they agreed, along with the management committee at Camden Road, that they should revert to the old model of having an honorary Superintendent rather than a paid full time post. The money that had accrued in the New Church Building Fund was redirected towards the upkeep and renovation of Camden Road, and the Fund was closed.

But new work was beginning. Mr Richard Jewell, whose resignation as Superintendent of Camden Road had indirectly led to Mr Lloyd's appointment, was not idle in retirement. From his home on Marshall Road, Wigmore he and his wife held weekly services for a group of local residents. The 'Tidings' for December 1945 reported that on October 4th the third Anniversary of the Marshall Road Fellowship had been marked with Rev Pike, and a few friends from the Tabernacle in attendance. It was also reported that a plot of land had been secured on which it was hoped to build a place of worship. By the time Mr Jewell passed away, in April 1950, the Wigmore Free Evangelical Church not only had its own building on Durham Road but also its own pastor. Rev E. Bickley was inducted into the pastorate of the new church in November 1949, and Mr Jewell's funeral was conducted jointly by Rev Bickley and Rev Pike. Writing in the 'Tidings' for May 1950 Mr Winfield listed the 'career' of Richard Jewell which involved serving as Superintendent at the Old Brompton Mission from 1903 until its close in 1913, the Chatham Hill Mission, and then Camden Road Mission from 1927 – 1945. This remarkable man of God, who was 74 when he died, had made a major impact on generations of people and had led several of these satellite congregations over nearly 50 years.

There was another interesting new work that developed over this period in connection with the Sunday School. During the Second World War when children were struggling to get to the Tabernacle, Mrs Doris Thomas, who lived at 584 Grange Road, Rainham, opened her home as a Sunday School. For several years this was considered part of the overall Sunday School of the Tab.. So when, in early 1946, there was a Sunday School Tea, it is recorded that there were 160 scholars present including those from the Grange Road branch. In August that same year the Sunday School outing to Margate saw 280 scholars, teachers and parents head off in six coaches from the Tab.. They were joined by a seventh at the Grange Road Branch at Rainham. The cause there finally closed in 1953 as other Sunday schools in Twydall sprang up, but Mrs Thomas and her two teachers were heartily thanked for all their hard work over the years.

From start to finish Rev Pike was an evangelist. In October 1947 he told a Church Meeting that he wanted to form a team who would go with him doing door to door work in the roads around the Tab.. A large part of the Church Meeting in April 1948 was given over to the topic of evangelism, and especially the need to reach men. The hymn 'Revive Thy work O Lord' commenced the discussion, while 'Rescue the perishing' brought their time to an end. In June 1948 he told the Church Meeting that he was looking to take a witness team into one of the local pubs one Sunday evening. Later in the month he joined with some Methodist colleagues to visit one of the pubs near The Strand, while in July he told the deacons he was looking to take a team into The Royal Oak on 11th July. At the Church Meeting that month he read from 2 Timothy chapter 4 and emphasised the words, "Do the work of an evangelist."Mr Pike also promoted various Open Air services during the summer months, and at the September Church Meeting "Our pastor called for earnest prayer that there might be more conversions in our midst." In October he started a Men's Contact Club.

Part of the motivation behind this evangelistic energy was a serious decline in numbers. The membership total had dropped to 267 by 1947 which was the lowest since 1890 and represented a 20% fall in three years. This was partly due to Roll revisions but also to a spate of deaths of older members which continued regularly throughout the decade. But it was the decline in numbers attending church that was giving significant cause for concern. A Covenant Renewal Service at the start of 1947 had seen only 160 out of 300 members return their forms. And even after two very good years of church growth Mr Winfield noted only 200 people present at the Lord's Table on May 6th 1951. This included "those who met around the Lord's Table at the Mission."

The fact of the matter was that churches everywhere in the Post - War era were seeing a marked decline in numbers. Patterns of attendance had been severely disrupted by the war and this had not slipped the attention of the Kent and Sussex Baptist Association. In 1948 they established an Evangelism Committee to look into the decline. The inspiration behind this initiative was Rev L. R. Barnard, by then the minister at Wellington Square Baptist Church, Hastings. The Committee's Report highlighted among other things "the problems of Sunday School leakage" as contributing to the falling congregational numbers.

One of the things the Committee recommended was the establishment of teams of speakers with evangelistic gifts to head up Crusades in churches where these gifts were in short supply. Mr Pike himself was one of those recognised in this way and over the next few years he took part in various Missions at churches throughout the Association. He visited Edenbridge (1949); Lewes (1950); Cheriton and later Portslade (1951); and West Worthing (1952). The encouragement Mr Pike received from these Missions he was able to feedback in the 'Tidings'. In the November 1949 edition he was able to report that as part of the Edenbridge Mission there had been 3 conversions; 7 who came forward for baptism; and 8 children who made decisions for Christ. The Mission to Lewes the following year saw 8 members of the Boys Brigade, aged between 14 and 20, come forward to make commitments.

This great evangelistic push by the Association was dubbed the Mid Century Crusade, and it involved hours of planning both at Association and local church level. The Crusade's key Bible verse was drawn from the prophet Habakkuk, "O Lord revive Thy work in the midst of the years," while the catchy slogan that was employed was "Each one win one"- an encouragement for each church member to bring one new person to church. Mr Pike produced a booklet for the Crusade entitled "Under Christ's Control." It was published by the Association in 1950, and apparently proved so popular that it went through several re-prints. Mr Pike served on the Evangelism Committee, and later on the Church Extension committee as well.

Naturally, given Mr Pike's enthusiasm for this campaign, Green Street was to have its own Mission. In fact it came in two parts. In March 1950 there was an Inner Mission which tried to draw on the church 'fringe'. For 7 days three outside missioners came and addressed rallies and meetings. Weeks of visitation and prayer meetings led up to the week, and the results were very encouraging. In September the second part took place. This was the Outer Mission consisting of visitation around the streets and invitation to evangelistic events. Again the results were highly satisfactory. In November 1950 the Church Meeting was informed that there were 14 candidates for baptism and church membership. In January 1951 there were 6 more. Mr Winfield's upbeat Report at the AGM in February 1951 stated that there had been 31 people received into membership in the past year, a total increase in membership over the year of 23, bringing the total to 315.

With the excitement and momentum of 1950, it was not surprising that 1951 should appear something of an anti-climax. Nevertheless, Mr Winfield was able to report an increase in membership over the year bringing the total membership up to 321 by the end of 1951. Mr Pike launched into plans for a second year of crusades. From the summer of 1951 plans were made for an Inner Mission in January 1952, and an Outer Mission in April. The format was similar to the one successfully adopted

61

in 1950, but this time the results were disappointing. Mr Winfield's Report in February 1953 reported a drop in the church membership total to 308.

Rev Pike was given the singular honour of being appointed Moderator of the Association in 1952. His address to the Association Meeting at Hastings that year was entitled, "Believers in Fellowship: the life of the local church." The Report that was given from the Mid Century Crusade Committee to the Association at Hastings said that over the three years there had been 124 Inner Missions or Crusades in different churches. This was to contribute in no small measure to the statistical increase the Association witnessed throughout the 1950s.

Year	no. churches	church members	S. School scholars
1938	81	10,867	10,630
1948	85	9,660	10,229
1950	87	10,035	10,976
1952	89	10,540	11,294
1955	91	10,869	12,161
1958	94	11,438	10,246
1961	100	11,936	8,706
1976	110	12,778	10,896

Between 1952 and 1961 the Association churches saw on average 330 baptisms per year. In 1955, however, there were 555 baptisms and in 1956 there were 433 baptisms. By comparison, in 1976 (the last year of the combined Kent and Sussex Association) there were only 179 baptisms.

One factor that contributed to this growth in baptisms and new church members in the 1950s was the Billy Graham Mission to Haringay, London. From March 1954 for 12 weeks Billy Graham preached to 11,000 people per night, six nights a week. Mr Pike made several contributions in the 'Tidings' during this period in which he expressed delight at the work and witness of the meetings. During the last quarter of 1954 Mr Pike held monthly evangelistic services himself at the Tab. while in April 1955 the Medway churches all rallied round a Relay of Billy Graham's Mission to Scotland which was being broadcast from the Kelvin Hall, Glasgow. Chatham Town Hall played host to this technological advance, and over the two nights there were 45 enquirers at the Chatham venue. Amazingly, the Tab. itself played host to one of these Relays on Good Friday 1955 when some 500 people squashed into the Tab. to catch a glimpse of the American Evangelist. Many were queuing for three quarters of an hour to get a seat.

Perhaps the major development during Mr Pike's ministry, however, was the initiative to plant a new church on the outskirts of Gillingham. As part of its evangelistic strategy, the Kent and Sussex Association had formed, in the Post-War period, a Church Extension Committee. Areas of new housing were identified as possible sites for new churches. The success of this strategy can be seen from the fact that in 1937 there were 79 churches in the K&S Association but by 1960 there were 100. Encouraged by the Association, Gillingham Baptist Church began to observe the developments on what became known as the Twydall estate.

As early as January 1947 Mr Pike told the deacons "of the possibility of securing a site for a Baptist Church on the Watling Street near Pump Lane, Rainham". In April this was taken to the Church Meeting under an item: "Possible Church Extension."

"The pastor reported that on a government order a Diocesan Church reconstruction committee had been set up. He had attended this committee and when sites for new churches were being allotted, had thought it wise to earmark one in Rainham (possibly at junction of Hawthorn Avenue and Begonia Avenue) for Baptist extension."

From that point on the wheels ground very slowly. The Borough Surveyor was involved in identifying the exact plot of land available for the site. The Baptist Church attempted to start a Sunday School on the estate. This was hampered by an unwillingness of local schools to provide accommodation, and in the end it happened out of the home of Mr and Mrs Larkins. The real anxiety for the Tab. was the fact that any building scheme was going to involve them in considerable expense. And the early 1950s did not prove a very propitious time for this because they had just stepped out in faith to purchase a new church manse.

At a Church Meeting in April 1951 Mr William Senior asked the pastor how the manse was fairing after the recent spell of bad weather. Mr Pike informed the meeting that most of the rooms in 59 Rock Avenue had leaks but that the back portion of the manse was particularly bad. A report on the manse a year later concluded that the damp issues could not be resolved without major expenditure, and the professional recommendation was to sell the house. On 30th May 1952 Mr Pike gave the deacons details of a house at 1 Brasenose Road which was advertised for sale at £3150. The deacons brought a recommendation to the Church Meeting in June that year to sell the Rock Avenue property and purchase 1 Brasenose Road. The recommendation was passed "by a large majority." The old manse eventually sold for £1,750. The new manse was purchased for £2,900, and the Pike family moved in during September 1952. Their family had been expanded in March 1948 when the Pike's adopted a boy and named him David Russell Pike.

Even with loans from church members the church had to take out a significant overdraft with the bank to pay for the new house. This makes the decision the church took on 18th November 1952 all the more remarkable. Asked to decide whether the Tab. should formally commit itself to the establishment of a new church on Twydall, the meeting voted unanimously to step out in faith as their forefathers had done. The 'Tidings' for December contained an article by Mr Pike in which he outlined in considerable detail the geography of the proposed Twydall estate.

In March 1953 there was some good news with regard to Twydall. The town council were only asking £500 for the site of the church. The Association had allocated £1,500 for the work which meant that the building fund already had a £1,000 start. In April the Church Meeting approved the Baptist Union Corporation as sole trustee of the land and buildings at Twydall.

In May 1953 the deacons started to look at building designs for the new Baptist Church. The July Deacons Meeting considered photographs of recent church buildings which Dr Ernest Payne, the B.U. General Secretary, had sent them. But the church was in no financial position to start anything. By October 1953 their debt was just over £1200. This was mainly as a result of the purchase of the new manse, but they had also had to pay out over £300 on a new roof for the Camden Road Mission. A Gift Day that month, to coincide with the pastor's 8th Anniversary, was to be divided between repayment of the debt and the Twydall Baptist Church Building Fund. By February 1954 large strides had been made. The debt had been reduced to £890 while the new Building Fund had £240.

Throughout 1954 various fund raising events were held, the main one being a Garden Party at Barnsole House in July. The event was designed to celebrate the church's 75th Anniversary, and it made over £120 profit from the various stalls. By November 1954 Mr H.H. Thomas, the financial secretary, was able to announce that the church debt had been reduced to £446.

The purchase of the Begonia Avenue site was not completed until September 1954. A Special Church Meeting in December that year considered plans for the new building. They were submitted by Mr A. Wright. One of the ideas was for a pre-fabricated structure. This had the advantage of being fairly cheap, and would have put an initial building on the site. But the Borough Engineer rejected this scheme. In June 1955 an estimate for a proper building on the Begonia Avenue site was in the region of £5,300 plus 6% architects fees.

Another major innovation at this period was the commencement of a Boys Brigade Company. The church had long been anxious about proper provision for young people. Over many years there had been consideration given to opening a Scout Troop. The deacons had consistently rejected this idea, but in November 1951 a motion to open a Scout Troop was brought to the Church Meeting by Mr Alfred Stanley. The motion was defeated 10 votes to 20. In November 1954, however, Mr Pike brought his own recommendation that a Boys Brigade Company be started at the Tabernacle. He had been encouraged in this by the Association. A meeting at Gravesend Baptist Church had shared the encouragements several Baptist Churches in the Association had received from starting Boys Brigade Companies. The Sunday School Teachers at the Tab. considered this a good idea, and so did the deacons. A fortnight later the Church Meeting also gave this initiative their seal of approval.

In February 1955 the Boys Brigade Company at the Tabernacle was formed. Mr John Wicks was the Company Captain. On the first night 8 boys attended, and on the second night there were 12. The Boys Brigade Rules were attached to the Deacons minutes for that month. They stated that the Company was initially for boys aged between 12 and 18; that smoking among members of the Boys Brigade was strongly discouraged; and that members should be total abstainers! The first Brigade Enrolment Service took place on Sunday 5th June. This happened to be Mr Pike's last Sunday as minister of Gillingham Baptist Church.

Mr Pike had given his resignation to the deacons in March 1955. He had received a call to the pastorate of Twynholm Baptist Church, Fulham. At that March meeting Mr Pike told the deacons of "his pleasure at the happy fellowship that had existed" during his tenure of office. He went on to say, "Several years back good results had been seen, but that was not so now", and he thought that "a change of voice might bring back the longed for results."

The statistics confirm that after the growth between 1949 and 51, when the membership peaked at 321, there was subsequently a year on year drop in membership until in 1955 it reached 247. Mr Pike had sensed this for some time, and at a deacons meeting in June 1954 he told his colleagues, under an item "spiritual welfare of the church," that "we were declining spiritually". All this was clearly a disappointment to the pastor, and contributed in no small measure to his decision to move on. It must have been very gratifying for him, therefore, to be able to conduct a baptismal service at the Tab. on his penultimate Sunday, and to be invited back on October 23rd that year to conduct a baptismal service for five more people.

Other changes were taking place at this time as well. Mr Winfield, the Church Secretary, made it quite clear that he did not want to face another Pastoral Vacancy. The task was too onerous. He had already been struggling with deafness, and had, for that reason, handed over the role as minute-taker at deacons meetings in May 1952. The solution that was proposed in March 1955 was that Mr Winfield should carry on as Church Secretary but with an assistant, Mr John Buttfield. By 1956 it was decided to reverse these roles. Mr Buttfield became the Church Secretary and Mr Winfield his assistant. A new Church Meeting minute-taker, Mrs Dorothy

Ellis, was also appointed. Mr Winfield was elected a Life Deacon in September 1956.

Other links with the past were being severed. In March 1955 the death at the age of 86 of Mr J.H. Ward was announced. Mr Ward had been Church Secretary between 1926 and 1939 before moving down to Portsmouth. Fulsome tributes to him were paid in the local press and by Mr Winfield in 'The Tidings'. Mr Ward had received an MBE in 1914 for his work with the Grand Fleet.

In July 1955 there were 40 people from the Tab. who made the journey to London for Mr Pike's Induction Service. In a final piece for the 'Tidings' in July he expressed thanks for those who had made the journey, and added that on his first Sunday as minister at Twynholm there had been 4 decisions for Christ.

On July 24th 1955 the Tab. witnessed its first ever Ordination Service when Stanley Feltham, whose father was minister at Borstal Baptist Church, was set apart for Christian ministry. Stanley, who had been a member at Green Street for several years before training at Spurgeon's College, was inducted as minister of Oxford Road Baptist Church, West Hartlepool in the September. He subsequently took on the pastorate at Tangier Road, Portsmouth before returning to Medway in 1965 when he took charge of his father's old church at Borstal. Stan Feltham was to have a hugely significant ministry throughout what became the Kent Baptist Association.

Jack Pike stayed at Twynholm until 1962 after which he had a twelve year pastorate at Folkestone. During that time he made occasional visits back to Green Street, preaching for example at the Church Anniversary in 1971. In 1974 he took on a final pastorate in Harrogate. During the Gillingham Baptist Church Centenary year of 1979 Jack Pike was one of the guest speakers. Members of the Gillingham congregation also made generous contributions to a retirement collection for him and Marjorie organised by the Harrogate Baptist Church. In retirement Jack and Marjorie moved to the East Midlands where he exercised oversight of Beacon Baptist Church, Arnold, in Nottinghamshire. He died in June 1993 aged 79.

In 1975 the Baptist Men's Movement opened twelve self-contained flats next to Twydall Baptist Church. As a mark of deep respect for pioneering the Baptist cause at Twydall, they named the complex "Pikefields". The name combined the two men who had played such a large part in the creation of the Baptist cause at Twydall: C.J. Pike who first had the vision, and J.W. Winfield who had been one of the early and generous supporters of the cause. "Pikefields", on Sturry Way, continues to serve the community in Twydall today albeit under different management and different ownership.

New Brompton 1866

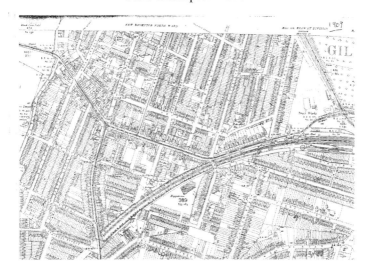

New Brompton 1909

I

Mr William Foster,
Founder member

Rev Frederick Edward
Blackaby 1855 - 1929

Mr George Hambrook Dean,
Sittingbourne Baptist Church

Rev Charles Haddon
Spurgeon 1834 - 1892

Original church building on current site 1881 - 1888

Young Men's Bible Class 1888

III

Fund raising Bazaar in old schoolroom 1880s

John Wills' design 1885   Revised design 1888

One of three surviving letters from Spurgeon to Blocksidge

Mr J.W. Nearn at a delegates'
conference of K&S Assoc. 1883

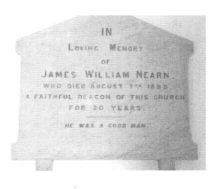

Memorial to James Nearn

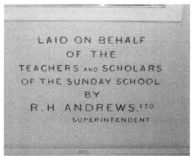

Memorial stones laid for the 1881 and 1888 buildings respectively

Memorial stones laid by Mrs Dean & Mrs Blocksidge for the
extension at the rear of the site in 1900

Mr W.A. Dyke, Secretary
1899 - 1926

Mr S.J. Strugnell, Treasurer
1884 - 1912

R.H. Andrews, Sunday School
Superintendent 1885 - 1894

John Rogers, Sunday School
Superintendent 1903 - 1907

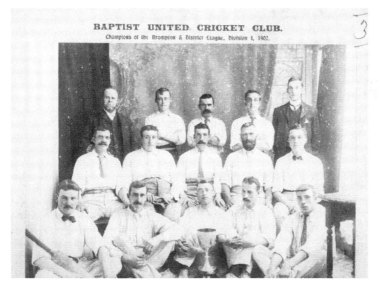

Baptist Cricket Club 1902:
Top row, far right – Mr E. Blocksidge
Middle row, far right – Mr F. Blocksidge

View of Tabernacle from
across the road

No. 2 and No. 4 Green Street

Bible Class outing to Tonbridge, August 1910

VIII

Front of church 1890s before organ installed

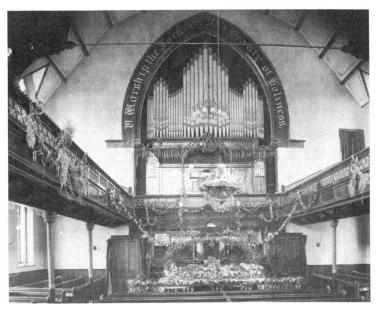

Front of church after organ installed in 1900

IX

Deacons and Minister December 1911
Back: Messrs Brown, Strugnell, Blocksidge, Dyke & Thompson
Front: Messrs Woods, Rich, Fieldgate & Jobling

Deacons and Minister June 1922
Back: Messrs Mason, Dyke, Fuller & Gordon. Centre: Messrs Woods,
Sanders, Blocksidge & Crawford. On the floor: Mr F Huxstep

X

Church used as Soldiers' Rest Room, First World War

Servicemen with Mr Blocksidge and lady helpers: August 1917

Mr & Mrs Blocksidge

Rev Walter William
Blocksidge 1850 - 1937

First World War Memorial

Rev Blocksidge and
Rev William Thomas Reynolds

Memorial to W.W. Blocksidge

Oriental Bazaar October 1927

Mr John Hyde Nicholson,
Church Organist for over
fifty years.
Photograph taken at the choir outing to
Broadstairs May 1926

Dickens' Bazaar October 1930

Mr Reynolds and the Institute: Gundulph League Division II Champions
for third year running in 1934/5 - Darts, table tennis, draughts and billiards.

Rev L. Reginald Barnard

Rev Cecil J. Soar

BAPTISTS AT LUNCHEON.—MEMBERS of the Baptist Tabernacle, Gillingham, gave a luncheon to the President of the Baptist Union (the Rev. F. J. H. Humphrey, D.S.O.) on Monday, the second day of their Diamond Jubilee celebrations.

Church Diamond Anniversary 1939: "Baptists at luncheon" from the 'Rochester and Gillingham News' 31st March 1939

XV

Deacons and Minister 1939
Standing: Messrs Bennet, Yeman, Langford & Follett.
Seated: Messrs Gordon, Ward, Soar, Tranah, Winfield & Jewell

Second World War
Memorial plaque

Servicemen and women
who died 1939 – 1945

Rev C. Jack Pike

Mr J.E. Winfield,
Secretary 1939 - 1956

Ladies Outing to Wannock Gardens

A meal for leaders and wives of Camden Road and the Tab.

Garden Party at Barnsole House August 1953

Marjorie and Jack Pike 1979

Marjorie and Jack Pike

One of many 21st Birthday parties held in the old schoolroom.
This was Peter Ousley's 'Coming of age'.

The Tab. Sunday School (with banner) 1950s

Induction tea for Rev F.J. Mason 1956

Deacons and Minister February 1959
Back: H.H. Thomas, A.W. Hardy, S.S. Yeman, J.E. Winfield, R. Butcher,
E.J. Walkling, W.R. Peck
Front:
W.G. Follett, C.D. Bennett, F.J. Mason, J.W. Buttfield, Miss M. Peck

Stone-laying ceremony at Twydall, 11th April 1959

Opening of Twydall Baptist Church, 19th September 1959

Inside Twydall Baptist Church 1959

Mr Buttfield
and Mr Winfield

The dedication of Ron &
Dorina Smith's daughter, Karen 1962

David & Audrey Rowland,
missionaries to East Pakistan

Boys Brigade with Captain John Wicks centre next to Rev Mason.

Girls Life Brigade 1959: Mrs Beryl Mason,
Captain, on far right.

Canterbury Street Methodist Church on corner of Green Street:
closed 1964; demolished 1966

Tom and Doreen Rogers'
Wedding 1956

Communion Service about 1965: from left to right: Sid Yeman, Roland Butcher, Stan Weller, Tom Rogers, Geoff Breed, and Reg Hughes

Ivy and Stan Weller:
Stan was Church Secretary
1959 - 1976

Christine and Reg Hughes:
Reg was Church Secretary
1976 - 1988

Re-Opening of the Tab after refurbishment
5th July 1970

The Dicky Dolphin Club 1969 or 1970

Aerial view of the church
with the cottages and the
Institute clearly visible

Margaret Helman and the Playgroup

Original artist's impression of the new Centre

The new Church Centre completed 1976

XXVIII

Rev Vivian Evans, Area Superintendent, along with his wife, Edna,
at the Centre Opening along with Doreen and Tom Rogers

Tom Rogers in playful mood

Doreen Rogers and Joan Johnson
preparing for Diners Club

Doreen and Tom Rogers along with children,
Pauline, Mark (left) and David (right) about 1975

Len and Daphne Millgate along with son, Ian

Easter breakfast 1979
From left to right: Hilary Shellock, Pauline Rogers, Hazel Mitchell, Sylvia Stevenson, Brenda Franklin, Miv Fisher, and Judith Harrison

Tony Beddows suitably attired

Group photograph at 1979 Centenary

Boys and Girls Brigade Company 1979 or 1980

Staff team: from left to right
Linda Nodder, Angela Flay, David Howlett,
Glynis Davey and Margaret Jonas

Margaret and Michael
Jonas

Phillip and Gloria Landgrave
with two of their sons

Doreen and Tom at
Pauline's wedding 1981

Tom with granddaughter,
Maria in 1983

Colin and Jenny Beadle 1965

Daphne Abbot
1978

Ken and Glynis Davey
1984

Joe and Rachel Davis 1984
with Rachel's parents
John and Jill Rowland

The GBC Couples Club

The GBC Couples Club

Ted and Nora Andrews 2006

Rogers House:
Memorial
to Tom and Doreen
Opened in 1992

Chris and Margaret Voke: first day at 28 Stuart Road
with Adam, Zachary and baby
Hannah

David Howlett (Secretary),
Lillian Smith (Treasurer) and
Chris Voke 1992

John and Joan Whitcombe

Jack Denness presenting a cheque for £2,400 to the Brigades after taking part in the London Marathon in 1991

Vera and Eric Paley

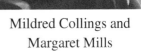

Mildred Collings and Margaret Mills

Len and Betty Jenkins' pastoral group

The Howlett's pastoral group

Hilary Cox's pastoral group

Camden Road Baptist Church

Camden Road Baptist Church

The opening of Walderslade Baptist Church 1990

The Wedding of John
Whitcombe and Miv Fisher
1994

The Wedding of Steve Barber
and Carolyn Hughes 1995

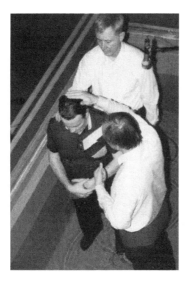

Chris Voke and Eric Seager
baptising Norman Chapman

Arthur Johnson
Church organist

Shirley Wenham and Dorothy
Marshall

Jean Millgate, Hazel Mitchell
along with Mo and Trevor Purser

Alison and David John
GBC Induction 1998

Alison the violinist

Dave leading worship

XLIII

John and Pat Buckley
with Jenny Matthias

Wedding of Adam and
Susanna Voke July 2000

Russ and Lyn Noble, Jenny Matthias, Dave
and Alison John, Roy and Jane Jones

Billy and Bev Gilvear

Lyn Newlan
Church Treasurer and Elder

Fred Adams
Church Administrator 2002 - 2014

Paul Clark MP with Rev Bill Clark,
founder of WOTS,
and Church Elder 2001 - 2011

Church Anniversary 2012

Brigade Camp at Downton Baptist Church 2013

Rev Stephen Greasley
November 2013

Ruth Millard
CAP Debt Centre Manager

Mark and Sarah Newnham with Children
Joshua, Amy and baby Abigail

XLVII

Architect's design for new church frontage 2014

Church Leadership Team 2014
Back row: Steve Powell, Adam Peak, Paul Wintle,
Albert Barnes, Jim Beadle,
Roy Jones, Martin Green, Steve Carr, Joy David
Front Row: Hilary Cox, Stephen Greasley, Lyn Newlan

CHAPTER 7

THE BIRTH OF TWYDALL: REV F.J. MASON

Shortly after Mr Pike's departure a decision was made that the church should have a Moderator to oversee the meetings while they were without a minister. In the autumn of 1955 the Rev J.A.H. Getley of West Malling was appointed. This was quite an undertaking for Mr Getley. He did not have a car, and on more than one occasion had to leave a meeting at the Tab. early in order to catch the last bus back to West Malling. His first meeting was November 1955 which was to prove quite historic. Six deacons were elected at that meeting including the first woman deacon ever elected at the church, Miss Muriel Peck.

The church was quite dis-spirited at this time. There was grave concern over falling numbers. Mr Winfield told the Church Meeting in January 1956 that the membership had fallen to 247, but of those only 180 could be considered active. Debates were held at the Church Meetings in March and April 1956 to consider what steps could be taken to draw more people to the church. It was decided that a Life Boys section of the BB should be formed for boys aged 9 – 12. In May it was decided to form a Girls Life Brigade, and at the same time to form a Band for the Boys Brigade.

There was also great nervousness about money. In July 1955 the church still had a debt of £300, but they also had essential repairs to carry out to the windows at the back of the Tab. which was likely to incur them in a further £400 expense. How are we ever going to be able to afford a new building at Twydall when we can't even maintain our own existing buildings at the Tab. and the Mission? To make matters worse, the Area Superintendent had made it plain to the deacons that they needed to offer a financial package to any prospective minister significantly higher than anything they had been paying Mr Pike.

In March 1954 Mr Pike's annual salary was £350. The deacons recognised that this was inadequate and proposed that it should be increased to £375. But when the matter came to the floor of the Church Meeting that month an amendment was brought by one of the members that they should offer Mr Pike £400 a year. The meeting agreed to this suggestion by 35 votes to

4. Mr Pike was most grateful. In December 1955, however, the Church Meeting agreed a recommendation that the next minister be offered a starting salary of £500 per annum. This was agreed 73 votes to 8.

The search for a new minister was not smooth or straightforward. Names of prospective ministers were forthcoming throughout 1955 but none of those who came commanded any enthusiasm. But in January 1956 Rev J. Forrest Smith from Leicester preached with a view to the pastorate and at the Church Meeting on 24th January he was given an overwhelming invitation, 104 votes to 1 (with one further abstention). Rev Forrest Smith turned down their invitation.

In March 1956 Rev A. Gilmore was in the frame for the pastorate, but at the Church Meeting that month Mr Buttfield informed the meeting that he was no longer available having accepted a post in Northampton. The new Church Secretary was able to inform the meeting, however, that the Area Superintendent had recommended the name of Rev F.J. Mason. Mr Mason preached at the Tab. on 27th April and again "with a view" on 15th July.

Rev Mason was educated in Romford and had trained for the ministry at the South Wales Baptist College. Originally he had hoped to serve as a missionary to China, but the political instability there had changed his plans. He had been minister at Underhill Free Church in Barnet before taking over the pastorate at Bourne Baptist Church, Lincolnshire in 1951. At a Church Meeting at the Tab. on 17th July 1956 an invitation was extended to Mr Mason 87 votes to 2. Mr Mason accepted the invitation and he commenced his ministry at Green Street in November with a Recognition Service on the 14th of the month. Rev H.V. Larcombe, the Area Superintendent, gave the address. According to the Chatham 'News' which covered the story of his arrival, Mr Mason was 36 years old. He was married with two children, Peter aged 4, and Rosemary aged 8. Approximately 200 people sat down for tea at the Recognition Service.

Evangelism and church growth were on everybody's mind. All churches were suffering a slide in numbers. The Gillingham Free Church Council arranged an evangelistic campaign in which the Billy Graham film, "Souls in conflict" was shown in April 1957. The Tab. hosted this for three consecutive evenings during which time 50 people came forward to accept Christ or to rededicate their lives to him.

The 'Tidings' for May that year said that the Sunday after the Billy Graham film there was a baptismal service at the Tab. and four people were baptised. "Afterwards twelve more friends came and stood at the baptistery, six to declare their willingness to obey Christ by baptism and six to express their desire to accept him as saviour." On Whit Sunday Mr Mason baptised 10 people with a further baptismal service planned for the August.

In May 1957 a Girls Life Brigade Company was formed for girls aged between 10 and 14. Beryl Mason, the minister's wife, took on the Captaincy at the end of that month. By June the 'Tidings' reported that there were already 30 girls aged between 9 and 14 in regular attendance.

At the Church Meeting in July 1957 Mr Mason was able to tell church members that he had obtained permission from the Odeon Cinema to speak at the Saturday morning Children's Matinee. That same month saw the start of another new initiative from the pastor which was to hold periodic Sunday morning services downstairs in the Institute. This was for the benefit of older members who couldn't climb the steps to the main worship area. The first of these services was held on 21st July, and several more took place over the next few years. Mrs Thomas was arranging lifts for those who needed them.

The biggest evangelistic drive at this time came from the Evangelistic Committee which had been formed to address the decline in numbers. A scheme was outlined to church members at the July Church Meeting for the systematic visitation of specific areas of Gillingham. A letter from Mr Mason preceded the visit by a specially trained team. Initially 300 homes in the vicinity of Green Street, Camden Road and Montrose Avenue were selected. But this was expanded significantly later in the year to include more of the Darland estate, with 900 homes to be visited and 3,000 leaflets to be distributed.

The year 1957 proved to be a significant year as well for two young men in the church. Both Terry Gamble and Brian Lloyd were accepted for ministerial training at Spurgeon's College. Miss Sylvia Stevenson meanwhile was studying at the Royal College of Music.

In the 'Tidings' for November 1957 Mr Mason reflected on his first year at Green Street. He declared that it was the happiest year of his ministry, the busiest year, but also the most fruitful. Mr Buttfield, in his vestry report at the Annual Meeting in February 1958, was able to confirm Mr Mason's opinion. There had been 21 baptisms in 1957 and an overall increase in church membership of 23. There were 263 members at the close of the year as well as 9 people on the communicants roll. Twelve months later, in February 1959, Mr Buttfield announced he was stepping down as Church Secretary due to the pressure of work commitments. The following month the church unanimously appointed Mr Stan Weller to this strategic role.

One of the other features of this period was the excellent working relations between the Tab. and their neighbour, St Mark's Church of England. In December 1957 Rev John Collins from St Mark's had spoken at the Tab. to 120 boys who were present at a special school leavers service. A United Prayer Meeting was held at St Mark's in January 1958 when, according to the 'Tidings' "so many from all denominations took part." This United Prayer Meeting was repeated on the 29th March this time in the Institute with a focus on praying for "Spiritual revival and a return to God." The meeting ran from 6.30 – 8.00am and was followed by breakfast. At the Church Meeting in May 1959 it was reported that "Our pastor and Rev Collins of St Mark's have been meeting for prayer and discussion." The outcome of these prayers and discussions was an innovative adventure in ecumenical relations in which St Mark's would close their evening service once a month and join worshippers at the Tab.. The Rev Collins would preach at the Tab. on that occasion. The following month this would be reciprocated with the Tab. closing their evening service and joining the congregation at St Mark's. Rev Mason would preach on that occasion. In December 1959 the two churches carried out this same exchange arrangement on respective Sundays.

The most significant event in Mr Mason's ministry was the progress of the cause at Twydall, and the eventual construction of the Twydall Baptist Church building on Begonia Avenue. The Association Extension Committee meeting on 25th July 1957 formally asked Gillingham Baptist

Church to form a branch church at Begonia Avenue. They again reiterated their promise of financial assistance and pledged to make the cause at Twydall the Association Church Project for 1959-60. The Church Meeting in September 1957 agreed (77 votes to 3) to accept responsibility to build premises at Begonia Avenue.

The Church Meeting in April 1958 enthusiastically welcomed plans for the Begonia Avenue building drawn up by Mr Keith Lower, the architect. The construction allowed for one main multi-purpose hall which would serve as both Sunday School and Church Worship space. Questions were asked at the meeting as to why no baptistery had been included.

In June 1958 a Finance Committee was formed with the task of finding ways to raise funds for the new building. A Building Committee was also formed to look into the finer points of the building design. The Church Meeting that month also agreed that the new cause should be known as "Twydall Baptist Church, Gillingham." Mr Lower's plans were submitted to the Borough Council and by the July they had been approved.

At that point plans moved on apace. In December 1958 quotes came back from several building companies and the deacons recommended the Church Meeting accept the lowest tender from Messrs Norman West of Commercial Road, Strood. This was for £4057. But still the plans made no allowance for a baptistery!

Money for the cause had been coming in steadily. At the beginning of January 1957 there was £188.13.6 in the Begonia Avenue Building Fund. By the end of the year the total had reached £329.4.1. During 1958 various anonymous gifts for the cause were received. There was also a gift of £37 from Camden Road Mission. By November 1958 the Building Fund stood at £465.7.10. Interest Free loans from church members were requested, and some were forthcoming. A collection of threepenny bits was started for the Building Fund.

The year 1959 was to be a milestone. On 28th February a Turf Cutting Ceremony was held with Rev C.J. Pike being invited back to cut the first sod of turf on the site. The official Stone Laying Ceremony took place on 11th April with Mr Winfield being asked to lay one of the stones. For the

April edition of the 'Tidings' the Financial Secretary, Mr H.H. Thomas, was able to provide a financial progress report. He had received £287 during the course of the year and in addition had been offered interest free loans from church members amounting to £375. A further £655 had been promised as a result of a letter sent to all church members appealing for specific financial assistance. Nevertheless, in spite of all this generous and sacrificial giving, and the huge financial support from the Baptist Association, the May Church Meeting had to give Mr Thomas permission to approach the Baptist Union Corporation for a loan of £1,250. By September the building was completed, and furnished, and on the 19th September 1959 the Opening Ceremony took place.

The guest of honour was Sir Cyril Black, President of the Baptist Union. The Area Superintendent, Rev Larcombe, was in attendance along with the Mayor of Gillingham and Rev & Mrs Pike. So well attended was the Opening Ceremony that some 60 people had to stand outside and hear the service through a tannoy. On the first Sunday there were 130 children at the afternoon Sunday School and 90 people at the evening service, mainly from the neighbourhood.

Mr Hulks was the first Church Secretary at Twydall, and Mr Buttfield the first Treasurer. After about a year the two men exchanged roles. The first Sunday School Superintendent was Mr Rowley, and Mrs Buttfield headed up the Women's Meeting.

Thoughts about ministerial involvement took place throughout 1959. Mr Mason approached the Borough Council to ask about the availability of a house on the estate to serve as a manse. They replied by saying that they would make a property available for a married couple. But at this stage the most likely candidate for the ministerial office was a single lady from the Baptist Order of Deaconesses. These were pioneering women who served across the denomination often in new post-war housing estates and initial pastorates. They were also paid substantially less than their male counterparts!

The Church Meeting in January 1960 was informed that Miss Marjorie Perry was available to serve at Twydall. She had done excellent work in her previous post and came highly recommended. On February 14th Miss

Perry, or Sister Marjorie as she was known, preached at the Parade Service at the Tab. in the morning and then again at Twydall in the evening. The financial package was a salary of £430 per year made up of £300 from the Baptist Union's Initial Pastorate grant (from the Home Work Fund), £65 from the Kent and Sussex Association, and £65 from Green Street. Mr Mason's salary had been increased to £550 in March 1958 when it was revealed that his wife was considering going out to work.

Sister Marjorie was invited to the pastorate of Twydall at the Church Meeting on February 16th 1960. She received 81 votes in favour with only 1 against. Her first Sunday at Twydall was 24th April, and her Recognition Service was on 27th April. In the June edition of the 'Tidings' she expressed her thanks for the welcome she had received, and paid particular tribute to the hospitality of Mr and Mrs Mason. She had found rooms at 69 Orchard Street, Rainham, but by October she was living at 19 Mierscourt Road, Rainham.

At the May 1960 Association Meeting at Bexhill Mr Mason was presented with a cheque for £1,000 towards the Twydall Building Fund. This was the proceeds of the Church of the Year appeal and represented the support from the churches in the Association. This still left a debt of £1,000 outstanding which the Gillingham church had to fund. A Gift Day in October 1960 raised £270 which reduced the Twydall debt to around £700. A further Gift Day in October 1961 yielded a further £260. By June 1963 the Twydall debt had been reduced to £291.

One of the other exciting developments during the early 1960s was the development of missionary links with Pakistan. At a Church Meeting in December 1959 it was reported that Terry Gamble, having completed his training at Spurgeon's College, had been accepted by the Baptist Missionary Society. In addition Valerie Shoults and Audrey Crane were attending St Andrews where they too were receiving training for the foreign mission field. During 1960 Audrey Crane married Rev David Rowland, and Terry Gamble married Valerie Shoults. On 21st and 22nd October 1961 Commissioning Services took place for the two couples as they prepared to leave for East Pakistan.

At the Church Meeting in January 1962 a tape recording was played (one of the first missionary tapes) of David Rowland detailing the early days of their time in East Pakistan. This was the start of a very meaningful connection between the two families and the friends back in Green Street. Letters and cards were exchanged, money was raised, and on one occasion Mr Mason managed to package a mountain bicycle and ship it out to Terry Gamble. The Green Street congregation had raised the funds for the bicycle and the cost of shipping it out to him. The January 1962 letter from Terry and Val detailed their culture shock in arriving at Dinajpur. They were also struggling with baby Alison. In November 1962 David and Audrey Rowland wrote a long letter with details of their ministry. Their daughter, Helen Mary, was born on July 22nd. In December 1963 letters from both couples were received. Stephen John Rowland's arrival was also announced.

In spite of an exciting first few years at Green Street things started to get sticky as time marched on. There was a constant anxiety over money. There was also a constant anxiety over falling numbers – and this in spite of a growth in church membership. Mr Weller's vestry report in February 1961 recorded that 70 members had made no appearance at Communion the previous year, and others had just attended on one or two occasions. Average attendance at the Tab. including Easter Sunday morning was 124. His vestry report in February 1963 recorded a fall in membership from 285 to 270 over the previous year. Average attendance on Sunday mornings for 1962 had been 114, and 76 members had made no appearance at Communion. In February 1964 Mr Weller reported that attendance at evening services over the previous year had averaged 104.

There were attempts to address the issue of declining numbers, and also declining levels of attendance. A Commission was proposed to look at the subject of conversion, baptism and church membership. But this did not seem to have the backing of the church leadership. Pressure was mounting on the minister all of which was compounded by some fairly turbulent and ill tempered meetings.

In April 1963 Mr Mason walked out of a Deacons Meeting when the deacons decided to move the date of Harvest against his wishes. There was a long running tension between the church and the young people who met in the Institute cellars. As far back as 1961 there had been consternation in the Deacons Meeting at young people in the cellars "holding hands etc" in the dark. The cellars were sometimes closed to the young people which didn't go down very well. At the same time there were complaints at lights and heaters being left on down there. In September 1963 there was a stormy debate in the Church Meeting concerning the heating and lighting costs of the premises and whether the young people using the Institute cellar should be charged. How often should the young people use the cellar and who was to decide? Propositions and amendments were forthcoming.

The following meeting in October appears to have been even worse. There were repercussions from Mr Mason refusing to allow someone to speak at the September meeting. The pastor had referred to someone's remarks as 'vicious' and in order to defend himself he had to vacate the chair. He began the December Church Meeting with the request that "a spirit of love would be evident in all our discussions."

Events at Twydall also took a turn for the worse. In October 1963 Sister Marjorie informed the church of her need to resign as a deaconess. Health issues that had dogged her previous ministry had resurfaced, and on medical advice she had to stand down. Her last Sunday was the end of December, and her Farewell Service was arranged for Saturday 11th January 1964. The speaker on that occasion was Sister Margaret Jarman, Organising Secretary of the Order of Baptist Deaconesses. Sister Marjorie stayed in Rainham and retained her links with Twydall Baptist Church becoming one of its founder members when it became independent two years later.

In February 1964 Mr Weller read to the Church Meeting the pastor's letter of resignation. He was taking on a pastorate at Tipton in Staffordshire. The March 'Tidings', which was prepared at the end of February, gave Mr Weller further opportunity to express "the deepest possible regret" at the pastor's resignation and best wishes for his new challenge. Mr Mason himself expressed himself satisfied that the seven and a half years at Green Street had been the happiest in his ministry. He felt there was a need to move at the current time in order to facilitate the children's education.

Not even this, however, was straightforward. Mr Mason's request to be allowed to stay in the manse until the end of August, and to be paid for this period of time, was at first agreed to by the deacons. But by the end of February it was discovered that Mr Mason was actually taking up a full time teaching post in Tipton, and that this position was to commence on 2nd March. Mr Mason's suggestion that he would be free to serve the church on Saturdays and Sundays did not seem to the deacons to warrant the payment of a salary since he would not be available for any duties during the week. Consequently at a Deacons Meeting on the 4th March, chaired by Mr Weller, the deacons recommended that Mr Mason's employment be terminated on 31st March.

This decision had to be taken to a Special Church Meeting held on 10th March and chaired by Mr W.R. Peck. The events surrounding the educational appointment were laid before the meeting along with the unanimous recommendation of the deacons. An amendment to allow Mr Mason to stay on until the end of August at a reduced salary (£260 pro rata) was defeated 26 votes to 41. When the deacons' recommendation to dismiss Mr Mason was put to the meeting it was agreed by 49 votes to 14. Mr Mason told the deacons that he was "heartbroken" at the decision.

The April edition of the 'Tidings' contained, under the circumstances, a very polite and courteous letter from Mr Mason wishing them well in the future and offering to help in any way he could in the next few months. On 3rd May he kept an appointment to take the Camden Road Sunday School Anniversary, and on 5th July he took the services all day at Twydall. The June 'Tidings' contained a letter from Mr Mason thanking the church for the cheque they had sent him. He and his wife were in the process of buying their own house. The Camden Road Church Anniversary that year, on 20th May, had been taken by Rev L.R. Barnard. The Camden Road people were delighted to meet their former minister again, his wife and two of their three children. Mr Mason's Induction as minister of Tipton Baptist Church was held on 14th November.

Mr Mason had been allowed to carry out part time teaching while in the pastorate at Green Street. This had been in lieu of having to give him a salary increase. One wonders whether this teaching appointment may have had an adverse effect on the performance of his ministerial duties.

Jim Mason stayed at Tipton Baptist Church until 1970 when he took over the pastorate of Ashmere Park, Wolverhampton. In 1981 he and his wife moved to Bristol where for the next 16 years he exercised pastorates at Downend and then Eastville. He died in April 2009 just short of his 90th birthday.

In May 1964 the church agreed, for the second time, to appoint Rev Getley as their Moderator. Mr Getley had taken over at Sittingbourne Baptist Church since he was last with them. In July there was considerable interest in the Rev A. Barry Blake-Lobb taking on the pastorate. He had been at Bournemouth for 14 years and while not an accredited Baptist Minister he came highly recommended by the Area Superintendent, Rev Vivian Evans. After the evening service on 9th August 1964 a Special Church Meeting was held. The meeting waited until friends from Twydall and Camden Road had arrived. A vote was taken and of the 112 members present Mr Blake-Lobb received 89% approval. The same meeting agreed to offer him a salary of £750 per annum, compared with Mr Mason's £600 per annum.

At the September Church Meeting there was great disappointment that he declined their invitation. There was also frustration that it had taken him so long to make up his mind. The Area Superintendent shared their frustration, but did recommend that they approach Rev Tom Rogers of Downton, in Wiltshire. Tom replied that he was unable to visit Gillingham before the New Year because his wife had just had an operation. The deacons did not think this was acceptable and so they proceeded to look at other candidates. On 13th December Rev W.F. Bacon from Palmers Green preached at the church. He seemed quite a plausible candidate until in the February he announced that he had accepted a call to a church in Northampton.

Tom Rogers preached at Gillingham on 21st February 1965. It was an inauspicious introduction. In a 'Baptist Times' article (7th January 1982) Tom recalled, with perhaps a somewhat clouded memory: "There were just 48 in the congregation and when the children left for their classes there were 20 adults left sitting at the back of a sanctuary then seating 750 people." Ordinarily this first visit would have been followed by a second preach "with a view". But the church members were clearly impressed with him. Comments about his "dynamic personality", and his excellent way of communicating to the children were made. The result was that a Special Church Meeting was called for the 2nd March, and, after only one visit, Tom Rogers was invited to take over the pastorate by 78 votes to 1. Tom's reluctance to accept the invitation was clear from his recollections in the 'Baptist Times' article, but he was encouraged by his Area Superintendent to take up the challenge. In April Mr Weller received a letter from Tom Rogers accepting the invitation. The news was announced at the Church Anniversary, and according to the preacher for the day, Rev H.W. Janisch, "A thrill of delight and satisfaction and praise and thankfulness to God ran through the congregation, and the whole very happy day was uplifted and lighted by the gladness of the people in the prospect of Mr Rogers' coming." (The 'Tidings' May 1965). Tom Rogers would commence his ministry at Green Street in the autumn.

Other changes were also afoot. At Camden Road the leadership of Mr Walkling came to an end in November 1964 taking them into a period of great uncertainty. While in March 1965 the church agreed that Mr Jack Jeffery, a lay preacher from the Congregational Church, should take over the leadership at Twydall. There were 51 votes in favour and 9 against. The debt on the Twydall building was cleared by the end of 1964.

In February 1965 Mr Winfield penned his last letter for the 'Tidings'. As Church Secretary and as assistant Secretary he had contributed a substantial monthly article for the magazine over many years. He decided that the effort of writing was getting too much for him. In March 1965 Mr C.D. Bennett, Life Deacon and one time Church Treasurer, passed away to the great sadness of all those who had known him.

CHAPTER 8

TOM ROGERS: PROGRESS AND A NEW BUILDING 1965 – 1975

Tom and Doreen Rogers were married in 1956 and served with BMS for four years in the Belgian Congo before moving to Downton, near Salisbury, in 1960. They came to Gillingham with a daughter, Pauline, and twin boys, Mark and David. Tom's Induction took place on 11th September 1965. The Area Superintendent, Rev Vivian Evans, carried out the act of Induction while Rev Frank Glover, Doreen's father, acted as chairman for the event. A number of the church young people had already encountered Tom at a youth weekend over at Warden Manor earlier that month. The Rogers' family moved into the manse on Brasenose Road, and thanks were expressed at the September Church Meeting for all those who had helped to decorate the property.

At the Church Meeting in September 1965 Tom made a bold beginning. He announced he would like the church to replace the 1933 Baptist Church Hymnal with the brand new Baptist Hymn Book. "This new book" declared the minister "is the best available and has been conceded a masterpiece." The boldness of this initiative was in large measure because Mr H.H. Thomas, the financial secretary, had already told the church earlier that year that they were seriously strapped for cash. The solution that emerged, therefore, was that all church members were asked to pay for a book for themselves and one for a visitor. This would involve each member paying £1, and it was decided that the deacons would make themselves available during October to collect the money at the end of Sunday services. By the November meeting they had received £118 and by December they were only £10 short of their target at which point it was decided to put in the order for the new hymn books. They would start to be used on 30th January 1966.

In the October 1965 edition of the 'Tidings' Tom encouraged people to pay for a hymn book because, he insisted, we needed the best material to worship God. His opening letter also quoted from Nehemiah: "The God of Heaven he will prosper us; therefore we his servants will arise and build." In many ways this was to set the tone for Tom's twenty year ministry at Green Street.

The November Church Meeting saw the launch of another new initiative by the minister, which was again fleshed out in the December 'Tidings'. This was the Stewardship Campaign. It was essentially encouraging members to consider what they could give to God. This included talents, time and also money. It was launched in January with a series of sermons. There were forms for people to complete and a Stewardship Dinner as well. The immediate effect of this initiative was to make a marked improvement in the weekly offerings. Between 25th October and 22nd November 1964 the average weekly offering was slightly above £30. Between 31st October and 21st November 1965 this had increased but was still just below £40. But between 30th January and 20th February 1966 the average weekly offering was around £54 while between 24th April and 22nd May 1966 it was £70. So that within eighteen months the weekly offerings had more than doubled. This level of improved giving was to allow the church considerably more freedom in the coming years.

A third innovation which Tom Rogers introduced within months of his arrival was a major overhaul of the shape of Sunday morning worship. Tom had expressed considerable unease at the teaching methods and material that were being used with the children. He observed that in the previous year only £15 had been spent on teaching materials. But one of Tom's strong convictions was that adults needed to learn as well, and the theme of education recurs regularly throughout his ministry. Discipleship required adults to engage with scripture and then seek to apply it. He wasn't convinced that normal patterns of Sunday morning worship allowed for that. Consequently in 1966 the church commenced what became known as Family Bible Fellowship. Originally it was to begin in the April, but it was put back until October 1966. The scheme involved worship starting with Communion each week at 10.00am (later put back to 10.30am). After thirty minutes or so the children would go to their groups. There would be no more than a ten minute talk introducing the morning's theme after which the adult congregation would break up into discussion groups studying the passage for the day. At 11.40am all groups and children would return for a closing act of worship.

This is a radical idea in the 21st century but adopting this pattern in the 1960s was very pioneering. While other churches at this period may have adopted some aspects of all-age teaching methods there can have been few churches that carried this out so comprehensively and for such a length of time. During the latter part of 1969 a Worship Commission was set up under Rev Frank Buffard, one of the church members. It was to look at, and report back on, several aspects of the life of the church, but one of its purposes was to review the effectiveness of Family Bible Fellowship. Clearly a number of people missed a 'proper' sermon on a Sunday morning! The Commission's findings did nothing to change the direction of the worship of the church, and the pattern of Family Bible Fellowship continued throughout Tom's ministry at Green Street.

One of the major changes that took place within the first year of Tom's ministry was the independence of Twydall Baptist Church. At a Deacons Meeting on 1st December 1965 there was mention of "an application from Twydall for independence." Tom agreed to speak with the Area Superintendent about this. At the Church Meeting in January 1966 it was agreed that Twydall should be allowed to form its own membership. Those members of the Tabernacle who wished to join the new church should make application to Stan Weller, the Gillingham Church Secretary. Those non-members who wished to join Twydall should apply to Mr Len Ashman. Tom Rogers was taking the service at Twydall on 27th February which was to be a service of Institution. The question of the Independence of Twydall was raised at the Maidstone District of the Kent and Sussex Baptist Association in January. At the Church Meeting on 15th February 1966 the names of the seventeen founder members of Twydall Baptist Church were read out. These included Jack Jefferey; Mr & Mrs J.W. Buttfield; Mr & Mrs L. Ashman; Sister Marjorie Perry; and Mr & Mrs H.H. Thomas. The transfer of this latter couple meant that Green Street needed to find a new Financial Secretary.

At first there was some reluctance on the part of the Baptist Association and the Baptist Union to accept this new church. There were concerns over its viability. Attempts by Twydall to send representatives to various Baptist meetings were met with confusion, and it wasn't until 1967 that the status of the Twydall Church as a separate fellowship was fully and finally recognised.

The subsequent history of Twydall Baptist Church does question the wisdom of this early separation from the mother church. It never grew beyond the initial 17 or 18 members. Jack Jeffery continued his work with the fellowship until the mid 1970s. Thereafter they struggled to find a leader until Derek Deavin provided 6 years as lay pastor between 1982 and 1988. A student from Spurgeon's College, Ian Birch, served between 1988 and 1990 until, with numbers dwindling away, the church formally closed in 1996. The remaining members joined Rainham Christian Fellowship under Rev Jim Crompton, who were given possession of the Twydall buildings. Since that time the church has made steady progress, and in 2014 with a membership of 24 they are looking forward to completing a £200,000 building extension to provide additional meeting room space. Peter Millard currently leads the fellowship at Twydall.

The minutes of Gillingham Baptist Church for the late 1960s also provide information regarding the formation of another Baptist Church on the outskirts of Gillingham. In March 1967 the Deacons minutes mention that the Kent and Sussex Baptist Association had declined to purchase land for a church building on the Parkwood estate. Nevertheless Sir Herbert Janes had offered to buy the land at a cost of £2,500. In May 1967 the deacons at Green Street agreed to contribute 30 shillings a fortnight for twelve months towards the cost of a student pastor at Parkwood. The student was John New, from Spurgeon's College, and according to the Church Meeting minutes when Mr New went to see Sir Herbert he was presented with a further cheque for £5,000 towards the cost of a new building. The first official service at Parkwood took place on 17th September 1967 in a local school. Fifty people were present at the first service. That number had doubled by the following Sunday! The church was formally constituted on 19th March 1968 with seventeen founder members, three of them transfers from Green Street. Tom Rogers conducted the Sunday School Anniversary at Parkwood on 22nd September 1968, and by the October of that year the improving finances at Parkwood meant that Green Street no longer had to contribute towards the cost of the student pastor. When the new building at Parkwood was opened on 15th February 1969 two of the Green Street deacons made a point of being present.

From a very early point in Tom Rogers' ministry there was concern about the condition of the Tabernacle, and an awareness that things needed to be done to improve the fabric of the old building. At a Church Meeting in November 1967 it was agreed to remove several rows of pews from the rear of the church in order to make a meeting place and a sound proof room as a crèche. This enlarged vestibule subsequently became known as the Conversation Area. In June 1969 side pews near the pulpit were also removed.

As early as December 1967 Reg Hughes outlined to a Church Meeting plans for a major refurbishment and redecoration of the Tabernacle. But it wasn't until the summer of 1968 that these plans started to firm up. In July 1968 Mr Derek Buckler, an architect, was present at a Church Meeting to answer members' questions. One of these questions was "Are these old buildings worth repairing or should we bulldoze and start from scratch?" The reply that was recorded in the Church Meeting minutes was, "Mr Derek Buckler considered our buildings were adaptable for re-development and also adaptable for future generations." He outlined the need to re-slate the roof, re-plaster walls and ceilings, and most dramatically to take down the old cottages and the Institute and replace them with purpose-built halls, an office and facilities. A guide price of £25,000 was attached to the scheme. The minister expressed the opinion that some grants may be available and loans could be obtained repayable over several years. Mention was also made from the floor of the meeting of the need for a lift.

Derek Buckler's "Survey and Report on Gillingham Baptist Church" was made available in summary form to all church members and was then brought back to the September Church Meeting. At this point it was made plain that in order to obtain loans from the Baptist Union it would be necessary for the current private trustees to resign in favour of the Baptist Union Corporation. Subsequently, after the routine Church Meeting on 10th December 1968, there was a Special Church Meeting "of the male members of the Church" which was required by the Trust Deed, to sanction the BUC becoming trustees of the Tabernacle, 2&4 Green Street, and Camden Road Mission. Agreement was obtained, and it was formally signed to that effect by Tom Rogers, and witnessed by Stan Weller as Church Secretary and Ken Barnes as Financial Secretary.

By July 1969 stage 1 of the renovation work (the roof and ceilings) was almost complete. The cost was £3,415, approximately £1,400 above estimate. Work on the interior of the sanctuary started on 20th October.

One casualty of this refurbishment was the church organ. Plaster was brought down from the church ceiling at one point and fell into the organ pipes. It became a major and delicate repair job costing some £800 and was eventually dealt with as an insurance claim.

The work on the sanctuary was completed at the end of May 1970 at which point the repairs to the organ were put in hand. The official Re-Opening of the sanctuary was fixed for 5th July 1970, but in order to reach that deadline a great deal of work had to be done to scrape the pews of paint and old varnish to which clothes became attached in hot weather. The place was also given a thorough clean, and the June Church Meeting passed a vote of thanks to Mr Michael Jonas for his team of volunteers who had worked so hard to prepare the room for the Re-Opening. At the subsequent Church Meeting after the Re-Opening Tom Rogers declared that "the beauty of the sanctuary has been much admired." The 'Baptist Times' for July 9th 1970 carried a feature on the redevelopment work and put considerable emphasis on the fact that so much of the work had been done by people from within the fellowship, saving somewhere in the region of £3,000 in the process.

Financing this major renovation was not easy. In June 1969 the Treasurer, Sid Yeman, died aged 81. Day to day running of the finances had long been handled by the Financial Secretary, Ken Barnes, but when he announced his resignation in the autumn of that year there was an urgent need to find someone who could handle both the day to day management of church finances as well as a major building scheme. In December 1969 the Church Meeting appointed Ted Andrews to the twin roles of Financial Secretary and Treasurer. Ted and Nora Andrews had moved to Gillingham soon after Tom and Doreen Rogers arrived. Their membership was transferred from Canterbury Baptist Church and by April 1966 he had taken on the role of Covenant Secretary, encouraging members to take out seven year covenants with the church in order that money could be recouped from the Inland Revenue. Ken Barnes had already put in place certain measures to raise funds for the renovation programme, and in March 1969 he was able to inform the Church Meeting that the renovation fund stood at £1,501.18.6. Of this total, £1,000 had come as a grant from the Norwood Trust but had a sting in the tail. Church members had to match that £1,000 within twelve months or the grant was to be returned. Small fund raising events were held: coffee mornings, sale of work, and strawberry picking. There were regular donations from individuals and organisations. The Baptist Women's League, locally and regionally, made significant contributions. In November 1969 a Gift Day was held yielding over £416 which meant that the £1,000 from the Norwood Trust had been matched. By January 1970 the Renovation Fund stood at £3,481.4.5

Throughout 1970 a series of fund raising events took place. In October a major 'Sale of Work' brought in over £350, and a sponsored walk brought in over £263. In 1971 and 1972 Len and Daphne Millgate held a series of coffee mornings for the renovation fund at their home in Gravesend. In March 1971 Ted Andrews was able to report that there had been a 15% increase in the offerings during the previous year as a result of which the church had been able to repay £400 of loans they had taken out to finance the sanctuary renovation. Nevertheless, he pointed out that the church still owed the Baptist Union over £3,000. A further Gift Day in April yielded over £150.

The 'Tidings' provided details of the slow growth of the renovation fund. Amounts added were £14.50 (Nov. 1971), £24.47 (Dec.1971), £21 (Jan.1972), and £10 (Feb.1972). The December amount was principally from a 'mile of pennies' fund raiser. The amounts from this point reflect the changeover to decimal coinage which began in February 1971.

But even while a debt still remained on the 1969/70 renovation scheme plans were already growing for the next phase which was the demolition of the old cottages and the Institute and the construction of purpose-built halls. By December 1970 the deacons had closed the cellars under the Institute because they were no longer safe. The Church Meeting in September 1971 had a long discussion on the appropriateness of taking out further loans to finance the new building work. It was widely recognised that repayments would stretch the fellowship, but equally widely recognised that the condition of the old cottages was now a matter of grave public concern.

In the Kent and Sussex Baptist Association 'Link' magazine for Jan/Feb 1972 it was stated that the two cottages were unsafe. "This property should have been demolished long ago but it was obviously necessary for youth work. Plans are now in hand for some kind of multi-purpose building to be used as a centre for senior citizens during the day and for youth work at night." The Church Meeting in May 1972 received a report from Reg Hughes about the new two storey building being planned for the site. Len Millgate was producing plans which would be submitted to the Borough Council, and both he and Reg were thanked for their hard work. By July 1972 fund raising booklets had been produced setting out the vision of the scheme and appealing for financial support. In November it was reported that £1584 had been raised during the year for the redevelopment scheme, and it was hoped that this figure might reach £2,000 by the year end. In January 1973 the 'Tidings' carried an article on the proposed redevelopment including a sketch of what the new centre would look like. It commented that architects had now been appointed to bring the plans up to the building stage. These were Brooks & Taylor of Ashford. In March 1973 the Borough Council gave planning permission for the work to go ahead.

Not everyone was convinced as to the wisdom of moving forward with the plans. Tom's article in the March 'Tidings' indicated there was a considerable amount of disquiet about the ambitious scheme. Moreover, the Special Church Meeting called in March to agree to take out further loans unusually went against the wishes of the minister. Tom urged the meeting to apply for an £8,000 loan from the Baptist Union, but others wanted a time for further prayer and reflection. In the end this view prevailed. When the decision came back to the May Church Meeting it was only agreed "by a majority".

Money was always tight. Shortly after the renovation of the sanctuary in July 1970 it was discovered that the heating system wasn't working. In November 1972 the boiler gave up completely, and Ted Andrews reported in the 'Tidings' for February 1973 that the cost of repairing the boiler had taken the church into the red. In order to get hold of a new vacuum cleaner for the church he appealed to the congregation for 69 books of Green Shield stamps! Nevertheless he was still able to report to the church in the autumn that giving had increased by 20% on the previous year.

It was remarkable, therefore, that at a time when every penny counted, and the church was on the verge of the biggest building scheme they had undertaken in forty years, a decision was also made to carry out an extension to the manse.

Central heating had been installed in the manse in 1966. In July 1967 Tom had told the deacons that he would like an extension to the manse. Nothing came of the request. In January 1971, however, the idea resurfaced with an estimated cost in the region of £800. In spring 1973 some remedial work was carried out at the manse along with a modernisation of the bathroom. Not until November 1973, however, did the proposition to extend the manse come before a Church Meeting. It had been a good month from a financial point of view. Ted Andrews had been able to announce that £1,600 had come in from the latest Gift Day which meant that £3,000 had been raised for the renovation fund during 1973. Flushed with this success the church felt emboldened to press ahead with an extension to the manse. Work started on 12th January 1974 and by May that year the Church Meeting was informed that the work was almost complete. Much of the work was carried out by men in the church, and the end product was a new study for the manse.

Meanwhile, there had been delays with the work on the new halls at the Tabernacle. In January 1974 the deacons were informed that Kingfisher Development Company had expressed an interest in partnering with the church in the new building scheme. This would have provided much needed finance and potentially a flow of income once completed. Nothing came of the initiative. In March 1974 there was another approach from Kingsley Smith Solicitors who owned the building on the corner of Canterbury Street and Green Street where the old Methodist Church once stood. Again, this looked like some form of shared building scheme. It was still being considered in April after which point it disappeared from the minutes.

A Church Meeting on 16th July 1974 received the five tenders from building contractors for the building work. The deacons recommended acceptance of the quote from Gransden & Co at £42,635. The minister invited members of the meeting to have a look round the dilapidated old meeting rooms. Ted Andrews explained to the meeting how the new work could be financed, and finally the motion to employ Gransden's was proposed by Eric Mountford, seconded by Geoff Andrews, and was carried unanimously. The die was cast. There was no going back.

At this point, as the harsh realities of what they had undertaken hit home, something like panic set in. Tom's article for the September 'Tidings' was upbeat enough: something is happening next door to the church! Demolition work had begun, the old cottages going under the bulldozer in August. Tom appealed for financial assistance from the congregation outlining the loans that they had so far secured. The Treasurer, however, painted a much bleaker picture. They would be borrowing around £34,000 on a £42,000 project. This represented around 80% of the overall costs. The weekly/annual repayments exceeded anything they could reasonably afford, and he was loath to have another Gift Day, preferring instead to have a Thanksgiving Offering at the end of the work and a Centenary Offering in 1979.

By the time the October 'Tidings' was produced the situation looked completely desperate. They had £5,000 cash in hand; loans of £8,000 from the Baptist Building Fund, £10,000 from the Baptist Union, £1,000 from Camden Road, and a further loan of £3,000. All this amounted to only £27,000 on a £42,000 contract. Tom had been confident of securing a loan of £15,000 which had fallen through, leaving a considerable black hole in the financing of the work.

Things looked a little brighter by December. Ted Andrews informed the congregation through the 'Tidings' that average offerings for the year had increased from £123 per week to £145. They had also received £2,000 into the renovation fund from the beginning of September. Tom had now managed to secure a £10,000 loan from Maidstone Baptist Church leaving the black hole at only £5,000. Articles about tithing members' income put more and more pressure on the congregation. By April 1975 the situation was, if anything, worse. While money had been coming in, and a £1,000 loan from the Baptist Association had been obtained, the building costs had increased. The project was now estimated at £47,000, and the shortfall had grown to £7,000. The 'Tidings' for April asked the congregation, if at all possible, to cash in any investments they had laid aside.

Meanwhile the building work continued with no guarantee of being able to pay the builders once their work had finished. By March 1975 the roof was on the new building and plastering was underway. David Bennett and Mick Keeley had installed all the electrical lighting and wiring along with a fire alarm thereby saving the church a considerable sum of money. Even the architect chipped in by reducing his fees from 8% down to 2% and being prepared to wait for payment until the end of the year. In the April 'Tidings' they were still in need of £3,000 to pay the final bill!

In May other members of the church used their training in carpentry and plumbing to finish off the halls. In July Len Millgate was starting to put central heating in the new halls. In September Michael Jonas again had a team of volunteers engaged in decorating the new rooms. The vinyl floor finish still wasn't down on 15th November when the Fellowship Supper was held. The following Saturday, 22nd November 1975, saw the official opening of the new building with Rev Vivian Evans, the Area Superintendent, again presiding. Even at that point the church was £1,912 short of the amount they needed, the building costs having again increased to £49,000. On the day of the Dedication of the Halls the sum of £719 was collected.

Once the new halls were in use one of the first tasks was to appoint a caretaker. It was recognised as vital to keep the buildings in a good condition. The first caretaker in 1976 was David Nuttall. In June 1978 David Howlett took on this role. Other changes of personnel were also taking place.

In March 1976 Stan Weller stepped down as Church Secretary after 17 years. Glowing tributes were produced in the 'Tidings'. Muriel Peck, the longest serving deacon, remembered how Stan had lifted the atmosphere of deacons meetings which prior to his arrival had been very formal and stiff. Tom Rogers himself paid tribute to the retiring Church Secretary for his faithfulness, efficiency, loyalty, kindness and love. "He has come to mean more to me than words can say." Stan effectively exchanged one role for another. In November 1976 he became a Life Deacon, the last one ever appointed by the church, and a Pastoral Elder with responsibility for visitation of the older members of the congregation.

Stan's role as Church Secretary was taken on by Reg Hughes. Reg had joined the diaconate in 1966. He had served the church as Youth Secretary for a number of years, and had served on the local Council of Churches. Reg had been instrumental in overseeing the plans for the new halls, and had been an invaluable member of the diaconate during that critical period. In June 1975 he was appointed assistant Church Secretary with a view to succeeding Stan the following year. In his secular work Reg was head of Lower School at Upbury Manor Secondary School. In March 1972 Reg became a Justice of the Peace on Tom's recommendation. At the same time that Reg took over as Church Secretary, Geoffrey Breed took over as registrar with responsibility for the Membership Roll and the Marriage Registers.

Quite a few people were disappointed when the new halls were completed. There had been an assumption that a lift would be included as part of the project, and when it transpired that this was not the case then considerable disquiet emerged. Consequently, at the Church Meeting in June 1975 Tom Rogers assured members that the installation of a lift was now the number one priority. Financing a lift, however, was never going to be easy with a large debt to clear which was why, in 1976, the Baptist Women's League (BWL) started their own Lift Fund. By March 1977 the fund had reached £1,000, and by October just over £2,500. An order for the lift was placed with Barron & Shepherd Ltd of London in September 1977. The price was £2,720. The building work was entrusted to A.T. Vincent and cost just over £1,000 bringing the overall cost of the new project to just under £4,000. By Christmas the BWL Lift Fund stood at £3,014 and by March at £3,896. Work began on the lift in January 1978. It was subject to various delays, and was finally and formally opened by Tom Rogers at the BWL meeting on 18th May 1978. Tribute was paid to the initiative and inspiration of the BWL in realising this long held dream. The BWL's next project was raising funds for pew cushions.

The repayments of the loans taken out for the building work were cleared relatively quickly. At the AGM in February 1979 Ted Andrews reminded the meeting that they still owed just over £20,000. A Gift Day in November 1979, the Church Centenary year, yielded £8,702, but by November 1980 the church still owed £5,200. At the AGM in March 1981 the Treasurer was able to report an increase in income over the previous year of 40%, and the outstanding debt had been reduced to only £1,641. This amount was finally cleared by the end of that year.

The year 1975 proved to be personally significant for Tom Rogers. He was inducted as the Moderator of the Kent and Sussex Baptist Association. This was an honour shared by two of his predecessors, Mr Blocksidge and Mr Pike. He had been asked to take on this role back in 1973 but had declined because he felt it unfair to be away from Green Street on Sundays. But when two Districts again approached him in 1974 he finally bowed to the inevitable and accepted the nomination with the encouragement and endorsement of the deacons. He became Vice Moderator in May 1974 and was inducted as Moderator in May 1975 at the Eastbourne Assembly. A coach full of people from the Tab. went down to the Induction and the deacons served at the Communion Service. Tom's term of office was particularly significant since it made the momentous decision to disband the old Association and form two new county Associations instead. The new structure was finalised at the 1976 Assembly which was held at Green Street.

Gillingham Baptist Church had hosted the K&S Association before but not for decades. It was a logistical nightmare with the need to provide accommodation for up to 300 delegates as well as meals and refreshments. Stan Weller master-minded the whole event, and the congregation at Green Street rallied to the cause, a number of people even taking a week's holiday in order to help out. It was a wonderful opportunity for the church to showcase their new buildings, and numerous letters of appreciation flooded in after the event.

Tom's year of office did indeed take him away on several Sundays, and was an indication of his growing reputation. The deacons had given him permission to act as Moderator of Gravesend Baptist Church in 1971 when they were looking for a new minister. In 1979 he took on a similar role at Sheerness. In October 1968 the Church Meeting endorsed his appointment as a governor of Barnsole Road School. In 1983 Tom was appointed a chaplain to the navy. On the wider denominational front Tom served as President of the Baptist Youth Movement, and was also a member of Baptist Union Council.

One of the features of Tom's ministry in Gillingham was his use of the local radio. He was a great believer in the power of the media to reach people who would not or could not attend a place of Christian worship. Details of Christian programmes on Radio Medway were regularly published in the 'Tidings', and Tom took an active part in broadcasts along with a team of colleagues in Medway. Not everyone at the church appreciated his involvement with the radio, and at one Church Meeting in November 1973 he provided a robust defence of radio ministry to those who claimed it was taking him away from his pastoral duties.

Tom also brought with him into the ministry an interest in and talent for printing. Before entering the ministry Tom had trained in the printing industry, and at Green Street he was able to put this training to good use. A print room was created in one of the first floor rooms off the back corridor, and many of the leaflets and brochures produced during this period were the results of the minister's handiwork.

Perhaps one of the most important of Tom's wider ministries was his role as chairman of the Gillingham Abbeyfield Society. In April 1967 he first shared with the Church Meeting his ambitions to purchase a property for the care and support of elderly Christians. The pastor and deacons were willing to act as trustees for this new venture. Christine Hughes served as Secretary to the new Society and Ken Barnes as Treasurer. The first house they were looking to buy was on Railway Street, but this had fallen through by the October, so that in November the Society purchased their first property at 4 Kingswood Road. Alterations needed to be made, and a cook/housekeeper needed to be appointed. Abbeyfield House was officially opened on June 19th 1968 in the presence of the Mayor of Gillingham. In 1971 a second property was purchased, this time on Barnsole Road. In 1980 a plot of land was purchased at Wigmore, just behind St Matthew's Church, and a purpose-built 12 bed home was constructed which was up and running by October that year. The Abbeyfield vision continued to grow, however, and at a Church Meeting in May 1985 Christine Hughes outlined the dream of an extra-care home for frail elderly in the vicinity of the Wigmore home. Christine continued as Hon. Company Secretary until the formation of the Abbeyfield Kent Society.

Abbeyfield was not the only Christian social enterprise that came under the auspices of the church. In May 1972 the 'Tidings' carried an article about Colin and Jenny Beadle's decision to sell their home on Barnsole Road to purchase 'Sunnyside', 24 Livingstone Road, as an after-care home for people with psychiatric problems. It would be a Christian family home for the residents. In May 1974 a committee of management was set up to help with the running of the home, and regular updates were brought to Church Meetings. The home functioned for many years and proved a haven to a number of people with special needs, some of whom found their way into the worshipping life of the church.

For a number of years two other church families, the Seagers and the Hodgkinsons, experimented with New Testament style group living. They purchased 187 Rock Avenue, at one time the St Augustine's vicarage and later owned by John and Pat Buckley. 'Cornerstone' was used as an example of shared community life.

There were innumerable changes of personnel during Tom Rogers' first ten years. On 1st July 1968 Jimmy Winfield passed away in the All Saints Hospital. He had given up his home on Chester Road some while before to take up residence in a supported unit over in Rochester. The September edition of the 'Tidings' contained an "In Memoriam" to Mr Winfield penned by Geoffrey Breed. It listed the various offices he had held at the Tab. as well as his career at the Admiralty in Chatham Dockyard. It was an affectionate tribute to a man who had given a lifetime of service to the church he adored. In March 1969 old Mr Follett, Life Deacon and former Sunday School Superintendent, passed away. He had celebrated his 99th birthday on 23rd December, and in recent years had submitted short pieces for the 'Tidings'. Sid Yeman, the Treasurer, died in the June that year, and his widow, Laura, in the October. She had been a member for 65 years. Mr Hyde Nicholson also passed away in 1969. He had been the church's long standing organist and was a veteran of the First World War. In June 1971 Miss Lily Owen died and left the church a legacy. She had wanted it to provide the church with a lift, but in the end it was used to buy recording equipment so that elderly members could hear church services in their own homes. This was a ministry that was greatly valued and which the church developed considerably over the next few years especially through Mike and Lyn Newlan.

In 1972 Beryl Breed stepped down as Sunday School Superintendent after fifteen years. The Sunday School had grown throughout these years, underpinned by a committed teaching staff and a variety of imaginative Sunday School excursions, often by train. Beryl was replaced by John Hodgkinson. Brinley Morgan took on the role briefly followed by Ken and Violet Sharpe, until Nora Andrews became Superintendent in 1981. Les Bennett was succeeded as Boys Brigade Captain by Barry Stedman. In 1980 Ron Smith took on the captaincy for a second time. Maureen Purser replaced Margaret Bennett as Girls Brigade Captain in 1975.

At Camden Road the work carried on quietly. Ray Mizon acted as lay pastor before eventually going to take over Napier Road Pentecostal Church. Roland Butcher served as Secretary. David Harmer held the fort for a number of years, becoming lay pastor in 1980. In this he was ably assisted by Jean Millgate as Camden Road Secretary. Alan Scantlebury succeeded David when he moved away to Newbury.

There was a solid core in the diaconate throughout Tom's first twelve years. Geoffrey Breed, Roland Butcher, Alf Hardy, Muriel Peck, Eddie Walkling and Stan Weller were joined in 1965 by Reg Hughes and Ken Barnes, in 1966 by Bob Warren, in 1967 by Eric Mountford, and in 1969 by Ted Andrews and Michael Jonas. David Harmer was elected in 1972, Eric Seager in 1974, and John Hodgkinson in 1976. It was not easy to get elected, and some candidates were proposed several times without being successful. This was to become even more problematic in the later stages of Tom's ministry.

CHAPTER 9

REVIVAL: TOM ROGERS 1975 – 1985

From the very beginning of Tom Rogers' ministry at Green Street there had been a large and consistent number of baptisms.

Year	no. of baptisms	Year	no. of baptisms
1966	31	1976	18
1967	56	1977	52
1968	19	1978	47
1969	25	1979	64
1970	23	1980	41
1971	39	1981	40
1972	47	1982	31
1973	46	1983	35
1974	43	1984	26
1975	24	1985	27

This totalled 734 baptisms over the 20 year period with an average of almost 37 baptisms each year. Over such a prolonged timescale this is quite astonishing. A number of these baptisms were of young people who had grown up through the church organisations.

The children's work had always been strong at Green Street and through the 1960s and 1970s this really took off. Between 1969 and 1974 an annual Holiday Club was held, called the Dicky Dolphin Club. Invitations were distributed to seven local Primary Schools with some 500 children attending over the course of a week. Many of these children subsequently came and swelled the numbers in Sunday School. A large teenage Youth Group used to meet at 14 Cleave Road every Sunday night and from this group there were a number of commitments to Christ followed by baptism. In 1967 thirty young people from Green Street went over to Holland as part of a joint Summer School with their Dutch counterparts. The following Easter the Dutch youngsters made the return visit to Gillingham.

Growth in church membership figures over this same period reflects a similar remarkable revival. In 1965 there were 247 church members. By 1970 this had risen to 302 and by 1978 to 366. There was a sharp rise to 421 the following year until the membership total peaked at 454 in 1983. These totals were common in the Victorian and Edwardian period but represent something quite astonishing in the modern British era. In addition to the baptised members there were, in any one year, between 9 and 16 associate members who had not received believers' baptism. Associate members could attend Church Meetings but could not vote. Each year these numbers were included in the figures submitted to the Association and the Baptist Union. The statistical evidence makes abundantly clear that something very special was happening during this period.

Even the Marriage Registers indicate the growth that was taking place at this time. The Marriage Registers in the church safe each contain 100 certificates. Usually it took between 14 and 18 years to fill one of these registers but Book 11, containing 100 certificates, took only 7 years to fill (1972 – 1979) at an average of just over 14 weddings a year. For a Baptist Church these are unusually high figures and reflect something of the growth in younger couples who were attending or in contact with Gillingham Baptist Church at this time.

A Young Couples Club had been formed back in 1961 and for over twenty years its monthly meetings helped to nurture strong friendships between some of the younger families at Green Street. It was one of those invaluable building blocks of church growth which strengthened the congregation from within.

Each year, in addition to the number of members coming in through baptism there was also a number of members coming in through transfer from other Baptist churches. But an interesting feature of the late 1970s was the trickle of people who joined the Baptist Church from St Mark's. Unease about the ministry at St Mark's following the departure of John Collins to Dorset meant that the Baptist Church became a significant beneficiary. In 1977 Bill and Betty Green along with David and Margaret Howlett came to Green Street. Alun and Brenda Wintle came the same year. In 1978 Judith Harrison along with Arthur and Joan Johnson became regular attenders. John and Pat Buckley joined in 1979. Some of these

Anglicans subsequently took believers baptism. Others remained as associate members until constitutional changes in the new millennium. But from this group were to be found some key workers for the Baptist Church over the next thirty five years.

One of the direct causes of this growth in numbers, and particularly the growth in Christian conversions, was the adoption of the Evangelism Explosion course at Green Street. A Special Church Meeting in September 1976 to deal with the future direction of the church had highlighted three major areas of development: Pastoral Care, Christian Education, and Evangelism. Evangelism had been the topic under discussion at a church weekend in September 1977 which had been led by Frank Cooke. In January 1978 Tom and Doreen attended an Evangelism Explosion training course. They subsequently put on a training event for people at Green Street. In May 1978 the Church Meeting was told that teams from the church had visited 16 – 18 households sharing the Good News. The June Church Meeting reported that there had been 15 decisions for the Lord from EE visits. By the end of that year the number had increased to 28 people who had come to believe the Gospel through this particular form of outreach.

Tom's report at the June Deacons Meeting in 1979 indicated his belief that the church had reached a plateau and that there was a need to study church growth principles. A Special Deacons Meeting was held round at the manse in September and the deacons were each asked to study the booklet "Can British churches grow?"

The success of this strategy and the success of the EE programme in Gillingham led to the British and Foreign Bible Society holding a national Church Growth Conference at Gillingham Baptist Church on 28th and 29th March 1980. The event was sponsored by the Kent Baptist Association. The church had to provide accommodation for the 100 delegates. Later that same year, in September, Green Street hosted a national EE Clinic and again had to provide accommodation for the delegates.

At a Church Meeting in October 1981 Doreen Rogers reported that from the five EE programmes in which the church had been involved a total of 92 decisions for Christ had been made and 71 had joined the church. These were quite breathtaking statistics. At its peak there were 18 teams of three people from the church engaged in direct door to door evangelism with other prayer partners involved at the same time. In 1985 Doreen Rogers took a group of 15 people to Copenhagen to train Danish Christians in the use of Evangelism Explosion.

The 'Baptist Times' (January 14 1982) continued to follow the fortunes of Gillingham Baptist Church. "Church that took off three years ago" was its headlines on page 7. It gave a full page account of the Evangelism Explosion initiative and its success at the church leading to 97 baptisms in the previous three years. The article contained comments from Reg Hughes, Hazel Mitchell and Tom Rogers. It also highlighted the pastoral care model in the church with its 24 care groups. Drawing on Tom's recreational interest in boat building and sailing, the 'Baptist Times' declared, "Skipper Tom cares for his babes."

Evangelism Explosion wasn't the only evangelistic initiative adopted by the church. The Billy Graham Crusade in 1966 saw a number of people from Gillingham travelling up to London. Tom even took a coach of 50 pupils from Napier Road School. In 1976 the church received a visit from the 'Certain Sounds' team which resulted in a considerable number of responses and commitments. In 1984 the 'Down to Earth' mission with Eric Delve saw over 1,000 people from all over Medway and Kent go forward to make commitments. Over 30 people from Green Street made recommitments at the mission and 56 other people were referred to the church. Four nurture groups were started to deal with the influx.

The growth of the church can be seen from some incidental events. In November 1976 some 220 people sat down for a Fellowship Supper. In 1979 there were 280 people at the Fellowship Supper, and the following year this had grown to between 300 and 350 people. In the January edition of the 'Tidings' Reg Hughes reported that attendance at the Carols by Candlelight was such that extra chairs had to be put out to accommodate everybody, and on Christmas Morning three quarters of the balcony was filled as well as the main body of the church - and this at 10.00am! In May 1980 the 'Tidings' reported that at the Family Service on Easter Day Morning there were over 500 people present.

It wasn't just Sunday Services that were witnessing substantial growth. A snapshot of the health of the church at this period can be seen by the statistical returns for the various groups and organisations submitted at the AGM in 1985. These figures pertained to the previous year's activities.

Organisation/Group	No. on Roll/ Average attendance	
Playgroup	49	47
Couple's club	20	14
Women's Fellowship★	41	32
Diners' Club	84	84
BB Anchor boys	20	17
BB Juniors	18	16
BB Company Section	28	24
Girls Brigade	57	55
Youth Club	32	20
Sunday School	136	116

★The Baptist Women's league was re-named in the early 1980s.

For three years from 1976 a Chinese Church was also based at the Baptist Church, meeting on Sunday afternoons.

Relations with St Mark's Church continued in a very positive way throughout the 1960s with United Prayer Meetings attracting considerable interest and support. However, once John Collins left St Mark's in 1971 relations cooled somewhat. In November 1976 the Secretary of the Parish Council wrote to the leadership at Green Street to say that fellowship between the two churches would not be possible in the foreseeable future.

The numerical growth of the church was not always reflected in numbers attending Church Meetings. In September 1978 Tom spoke to the members regarding poorly attended Church Meetings. "Mr Rogers said that many times over the last months had quorum been called by a member the meeting would have had to be abandoned. A minimum of 60 members was required to conduct an official Church Meeting and this very often was not being met." The minister's rebuke didn't necessarily have the desired effect. Several subsequent meetings failed to attract sufficient numbers of church members to make them quorate.

The year 1979 was the Church's Centenary year, and to mark the occasion it was decided to have a series of guest speakers spread throughout the twelve months: Rev Bill Hancock, Rev Dr Raymond Brown, Rev Frank Cooke, Rev Dr Morris West (B.U. President), Rev Vivian Evans, Rev C.J. Pike (former minister) and Rev Dr David Russell (General Secretary of the Baptist Union). At the beginning of the year Muriel Peck came off the diaconate after 24 years. In the 'Tidings', Tom paid tribute to her "decisive thinking" and major contribution to the life of the church. In 1981 Muriel married Wilfred Hyde, and the following year she transferred her membership to Park Road, Bromley.

Even with the refurbishment of 1970 and the redevelopment of 1975 the old buildings at Green Street needed constant attention and repair work. In 1981 there was also a further major alteration to the platform and pulpit area of the sanctuary to create more space for dance and drama. Len Millgate and Colin Beadle also put in hours of work replacing the old lead-lined baptistery with a fibre-glass model. It was brought into use in December 1981.

Such was the reputation of Tom Rogers' ministry that Green Street was used as a training centre for various Christian ministry programmes. In February 1966 it was agreed that Gillingham Baptist Church would serve as a 'Time for God' training centre for the South East of England. Bill West was the first student. He started in summer 1966 at Camden Road which was in need of more consistent leadership. In 1980 Gordon O'Neill came as a pre-collegiate student prior to training at Spurgeon's College. The arrangement went well, and the following year Bob and Angela Almond came on a similar basis. In July 1982 David John came as a pre-collegiate student but in the end opted to go to London Bible College.

The church was also starting to produce its own candidates for Baptist ministry. In November 1972 Ian Millgate was recommended by the Church Meeting for ministerial training. Ian completed his training at Spurgeon's College. He was ordained at Gillingham Baptist Church on 25th June 1977 and was subsequently inducted as associate minister at Tyndale

Baptist Church, Bristol. Ian went on to have further ministries at Longbridge, Birmingham; and Coleford, Gloucestershire, serving as the Gloucester and Herefordshire Association Secretary until 1990 when he went to work for the ministry department at the Baptist Union in Didcot.

In July 1973 Geoff Andrews, son of Ted and Nora, was also approved for ministerial training. He had a pre-collegiate year at Worcester Baptist Church before entering Spurgeon's College. He was ordained at Green Street on 5th July 1981 and was inducted at Darnall Road, Sheffield on Saturday 11th July. Geoff had subsequent ministries at Wood Green and Perry Rise in London before becoming Regional Minister Team Leader for the London Baptist Association in 2011.

In November 1979 Geoffrey Breed took on the role as Moderator at Sittingbourne Baptist Church. His time there was much appreciated and in June 1980 the church invited him to take over the pastorate. He was inducted on 27th September, Tom Rogers conducting the service. Having previously completed Baptist Union theological training Geoffrey was approved by the national Ministerial Recognition Committee and was ordained at Green Street on 23rd May 1981. Rev George Beasley-Murray was the preacher. Geoffrey served as minister at Sittingbourne Baptist Church until his retirement in 1988. Geoffrey had first been elected to the diaconate at Green Street in November 1963, and the departure of Geoffrey and Beryl to Sittingbourne robbed Green Street of two of their most diligent workers.

In November 1982 the Church Meeting approved David Rogers for ministerial training. David subsequently married Susan Goldspink from Tunbridge Wells in April 1983, and they moved to Oxford in September to commence training at Regents Park College. David's ordination was at Green Street on 29th June 1986 conducted by Rev Dr Barrie White. David went on to have ministries on the Isle of Wight, Wokingham, Salisbury, the East Midlands Baptist Association, and now in Croydon.

The church was also producing its own candidates for missionary work. Terry and Valerie Gamble had returned from East Pakistan in 1965. David and Audrey Rowland continued in East Pakistan although the political and social instability meant that Audrey and the three children had to return to England for long periods of time. David finally returned from Bangladesh in 1973, and in 1974 took on a different challenge as minister of the Blackbird Leys Ecumenical Church in Oxford. He had subsequent ministries in Botley, Oxford, and then as Ecumenical Officer for Coventry and Warwickshire before retiring in 2001.

Brad and Kathleen Greening continued to serve in Brazil where they had been exercising a highly successful ministry for many years. Letters from them often featured in the 'Tidings' and they were very much considered part of the extended church family. They returned to England in 1984 and Brad became minister at Measham and Netherseal in the East Midlands. On their retirement Brad and Kathleen returned to Gillingham. They came into membership of the Baptist Church in 2001 before moving to Eastbourne in 2012.

Sylvia Stevenson spent ten years between 1966 and 1976 teaching at a Girls School in Kenya before returning to Gillingham. Letters were sent to her as a missionary from the church. In 1976 Hilary Shellock had a spell nursing in Nain, Labrador facing temperatures of minus 40 degrees. In 1977 Frank and Margaret Buffard went out to Spain where they spent several years engaged in missionary work before returning to the UK. Back in the 1960s Frank had written a very useful History of the Kent and Sussex Baptist Association which still remains a starting point for historical research into that subject.

In August 1981 Pauline Rogers married Mark Godfrey. In March 1982 they were accepted as missionaries by the BMS. Their daughter Maria Elizabeth was born in June 1983 and on 31st July that year they had their Valedictory Service at Green Street before going out to Zaire. They returned to England in 1987.

Lyn Newble had long been interested in Africa. She went out to Nigeria for a spell with Sudan United Mission in 1975. But it was at a Church Meeting at Green Street in March 1983 that she explained about her sense of call to serve in Sudan. The Meeting endorsed her vocation and on 28th August that year she also had a Valedictory Service at Green Street before leaving for Juba in September. The 'Tidings' for September 1983 had biographical sketches of both Lyn Newble and Mark & Pauline Godfrey under the heading "Our missionaries are on their way." Lyn became the longest serving of all the Gillingham missionaries. In August 1990 she married Russ Noble, and to date the couple continue to serve in what is now South Sudan. A trained teacher she has been employed principally in the areas of literacy training and translation work. Her close connections with Camden Road provided that fellowship with a direct link to the overseas mission field.

In 1982 the church approved Pauline Stutton to serve as the BMS representative for the Kent Baptist Association. Pauline subsequently went on to serve on the BMS General Committee. In September 1983 Brenda Franklin spoke at a Church Meeting about her sense of call to go full time with the Christian Literature Crusade (CLC). Brenda served in London and Southampton before taking on the Chatham branch in 2000.

The numerical growth in Gillingham Baptist Church brought with it an increase in income. This allowed the church to provide the staff with reasonable salaries. Tom's stipend ranged from between 20% and 40% above the Baptist Union minimum stipend. Increased income also meant that the church was able financially to support more of their missionaries, and there was a marked increase in the mission budget from the late 1970s onwards. In 1977 a Council of Mission was established. In 1980 19.7% of the total church income was given away in missionary giving, grants, and fees. This included a significant contribution to the salary of the newly appointed KBA Association minister. The increased income also meant that the church had money available to expand its own internal ministries.

In March 1976 Margaret Jonas was appointed and employed as clerical assistant to the minister. In June 1979 it was agreed to increase her hours to five mornings a week. When Margaret left the district in 1983 her replacement as clerical assistant was Maureen Purser. In June 1978 David Howlett started duties as church caretaker. In October 1980 his title was changed to Warden to take account of his wider duties and responsibilities.

In October 1979 Ted Andrews recommended to the Church Meeting that serious consideration be given to employ a full time assistant minister to help with the pastoral workload. It was recognised that with a church of nearly 400 members it was impossible for Tom, or Stan Weller as Pastoral

Elder, to deal with all that needed to be done. At the same time it was agreed to bring over Phillip and Gloria Landgrave from the Southern Baptist Theological Seminary, Louisville, Kentucky. Phillip was employed as a Minister of Music in his home church, and it was felt that his experience could be useful. The couple arrived in early 1980 for six months. They made major contributions to the church music putting on a number of performances including one for Easter 1980. Within a short while of their return to America, Sylvia Stevenson was approached about becoming a full time member of staff with responsibility for music and education. The Church Meeting agreed to her appointment and she started as Director of Education & Music in January 1981. The following month she also took on the role as assistant Association Secretary to the KBA.

Sylvia provided a number of courses for church members about aspects of the Bible and Christian living. These were well received and much appreciated. She had a major role in directing the shape of church music with choirs and new musicians. In April 1981 a performance of Jimmy & Carol Owens' 'The Witness' was put on at Green Street. At Christmas 1982 a performance of 'The Glory of Christmas' was also staged.

Not everyone was happy with the increasing profile Sylvia took in the life of the church. On leaving the church in 1989 she wrote of encountering unexpected discrimination on account of her gender. Her failure to get elected as a deacon created considerable difficulty for the leadership who needed her involvement at their meetings. In December 1984 her title was changed to 'Assistant to the Minister' allowing her officially a wider remit than the one drawn up in 1980/81. In May 1982 Tom was invited to lead the opening celebration at the Baptist Assembly. In the 'Tidings' he gave thanks to Sylvia Stevenson, Arthur Johnson and Karenza Beddow for lifting the vast congregation and equipping the choir. He was also grateful to Beryl Jordan who brought the Bible reading using her Braille edition.

The growing church brought with it a need to think in new ways and to restructure the work of the fellowship. The structures that had served a membership of 200 people were not likely to work as well in a membership of over 400. To facilitate future growth and expansion new systems of pastoral care and administration were needed.

Changes to the pastoral care arrangements came relatively easily. The church had appointed a series of Home Group leaders as early as 1972. In 1977 studies were made of other large Baptist Churches and the pattern of pastoral care they used. From the examples of Upton Vale, Torquay and Purley Baptist Church it was decided to arrange the congregation into approximately 25 pastoral groups of between 10 and 20 people. Each deacon would have oversight of three or four groups. In the autumn of 1979 the task of organising the pastoral care was given to Hazel Mitchell. By the end of that year there were reported to be 30 pastoral groups in operation. Over the next few years there were changes in the leadership of the pastoral groups, and some clearly worked more effectively than others, but the shape and structure remained broadly the same.

Along with these changes came a feeling that the leadership base of the church needed to be widened, and the participation of more members encouraged. The leadership frequently expressed unease at the potential bottle neck effect they could unintentionally exercise. The result of this, in 1982, was the establishment of several Boards to which the Church Meeting delegated responsibility. Initially there were six Boards – Finance, Camden Road, Fabric, Youth, Pastoral, and the Lord's House. A seventh one, Education and Music, followed soon after the others. The Mission Council was subsequently reconfigured to become the Mission Board which created the eighth. The Boards brought far more people into the decision making process, and streamlined the work of the Church Meeting.

In 1985 the Board Chairmen were recorded as follows:

Camden Road	Bernie Pinner
Fabric	John Buckley
Finance	Eric Seager*
Lord's House	Alex Russell
Mission	John Rowland
Pastoral	Ted Andrews
Worship and Education	Sylvia Stevenson
Youth	Ron Smith

*Eric Seager took over as Church Treasurer in 1981 following Ted Andrews' resignation.

The most controversial aspect of this attempt to widen the leadership base of the church and move to a more plural understanding of church leadership, was the plan to appoint elders. Hitherto the church had operated with a minister and elected deacons, but in an attempt to make use of the evident talent that was around at the time and to allocate clear areas of responsibility, the church leaders began in 1981 to consider the appointment of elders. The Church Meeting in October 1981 heard back from a Deacons Conference where the idea of the Boards and elders had been expressed. Changes to the Church Rules were approved in 1982 to allow for the election of elders. In January 1983 the names of six candidates for eldership were brought before the Church Meeting to be voted on in February. At the February meeting there was considerable disquiet that insufficient time had been given to the proposed changes, and a number of members were uneasy about the implications of such a major constitutional change. In the end only one of the candidates, John Rowland, was elected.

The failure to create this new tier of oversight was a body blow to those who had been working on the new structures for so long. The leadership had assumed the changes would be agreed and the Church Meeting clearly de-railed the plans. There had undoubtedly been a breakdown in communication and vision between the leaders and the members. In 1985 a second elder, Eric Seager, was appointed, but only a few months after this John Rowland was appointed to a Headship of a Community College in Brighton and he left the Towns. This left the church again with only one elder to work alongside the minister and deacons. The structural change that had been envisaged never happened.

By this time the seeming exponential growth of the church membership was being checked. Key to this was the government's decision made in 1981 to close the Chatham Dockyard. The Deacons Meeting in July 1981 noted that "31 folk connected with the fellowship will lose their employment as a result of the closure of HM Dockyard, Chatham." The mini-exodus started in March 1983 when David and Margaret Bennett moved to Devonport. They were followed by Brenda Dent and Patricia Lewis who moved to Plymouth. John and Janet Cole moved to Aldershot and transferred their membership to Fleet Baptist Church. In August/September 1983 Michael and Margaret Jonas left for Ivybridge in

Devon. Michael resigned as a deacon and Margaret as clerical assistant and registrar. At the same time Angela Flay left for Scotland. She had been involved in leading the Church Playgroup. Peter and Christine Warner left for Westcliff-on-Sea in September 1983. The following year saw the departure of two more deacons, Alan Scantlebury and his wife to Manchester, and Keith Stevens and his wife, Jan, to Stafford. Ted and Nora Andrews also moved to Bromley in 1985.

The failure to get through the eldership changes combined with the departure of some key members of the church leadership had a marked dis-spiriting effect on the life of the fellowship. What added to this sense of disappointment was the poor health of both Tom and Doreen Rogers.

In 1981 there had been a real sense of celebration as Tom and Doreen marked their Silver Wedding Anniversary as well as Tom's 25 years of ordained ministry. In May the couple travelled to America and stayed with the Landgraves. There was travelling and sight-seeing as well as some preaching. A celebration at the church in July saw over 400 people in attendance. The couple were presented with a Royal Doulton complete dinner and tea set. In May 1982 Tom had a month's sabbatical at Spurgeon's College studying aspects of worship in the Old Testament Temple and the synagogue. By the autumn of 1982, however, both Doreen and Tom had received major surgery for cancer. This took Tom out of ministerial duties for some considerable time, and on his return he was only taking part in one service per Sunday.

The deacons were unfairly chastised by some church members who maintained that they should have prevented Tom from over working, and should have kept a tighter control of his diary. Such criticism failed to appreciate the nature of the cancer from which Tom was suffering. In the 'Tidings' for September 1983 Tom confided that "cancer has reared its ugly head in Doreen again." She would need extensive chemotherapy. By the November Tom himself was back in hospital for more surgery. He said that both he and Doreen were at peace about the whole thing. In 1984 Tom and Doreen had been able to give their testimonies at the Baptist Assembly. The whole experience proved very moving to a lot of people. (See appendix 1)

But the spirit of tolerance and understanding that had marked the earlier period of Tom's illness was wearing thin by the time of this latest incapacity. In the spring of 1984 the deacons were having to fend off criticism of underperforming preachers. There was dissatisfaction in some quarters about the use of dance and drama. Numbers attending the evening service and the central prayer meeting had fallen off.

The work at Camden Road was also struggling. Jean Millgate wrote a very downbeat article for the 'Tidings' at the end of 1982. There was a shortage of workers. The committed core was getting smaller. Numbers were falling, and there was a malaise over the whole work. In February 1984 Alan Scantlebury provided another bleak assessment of the future of the work at Camden Road. The workers were "sagging" and there were "undercurrents of discontent". He was struggling to see what the future held for the Mission.

Then in March 1985 Tom announced he was leaving the church. He had received a call from the Baptist Union to head up a new department of Evangelism. Bill Hancock, the Area Superintendent for the South East, was leaving at the same time to take over the Ministry Department. While there was some considerable pride in the fact that Tom had been asked to take on this major national role, there was also a huge sense of disappointment that they were losing the man whose inspiration had overseen the dramatic growth and transformation of the church in the last twenty years. There was also a degree of fear and trepidation about what the future would hold.

Tom and Doreen's Farewell Services were arranged for the weekend of the 7th & 8th September 1985. It marked exactly twenty years since the Induction. Tom's final letter in the 'Tidings' thanked everyone for the adventure of the past years of ministry. He quoted the words of the old hymn "Forward be our watchword", and ended with his characteristic, "Bless you". Reg Hughes in the same edition of the 'Tidings' paid tribute to the fact that through the Reach and Teach programme of Evangelism Explosion over 100 people had committed their lives to Christ, and a further 100 people had been equipped to share the Good News. "If asked what has been the most significant feature of Tom's ministry in Gillingham," wrote Reg, "it is surely that he has proclaimed and lived the gospel of love; equally his ability to encourage others to work for Christ's kingdom, whether full time or part time."

Tom's ministry at the Baptist Union in London was short lived, although he did manage to pilot a project which was later run out across the denomination called Action in Mission (AIM). This was a mission audit of the life of the local church which proved hugely beneficial to a number of fellowships. In early 1987 both Tom and Doreen were in considerable pain with recurrences of the cancer. On 7th September 1987 Doreen passed away.

For many years after arriving in Gillingham, Doreen fulfilled her professional role as a teacher. She was Head of R.E. at Napier Road Secondary School and also taught P.E. While supporting Tom's ministry, leading a Bible Class, and involvement with Brigades, Doreen was also responsible for the Diners' Club at the church every Thursday. A Service of Praise and Thanksgiving for Doreen's life was held at Green Street on Friday 18th September. There were over 500 people in attendance, an indication of the affection with which she was held.

Tom had been booked to speak at the Gillingham United Service in January 1988 but in November 1987 he was back in St Thomas' Hospital for further surgery. He went to be with his Lord on 12th December. He was 56 years old. A Memorial Service was held at Green Street on the 2nd January 1988.

Rev J.J. Brown, who had been Tom's minister back in Erith, Kent, put together the obituary to Tom Rogers that appeared in the Baptist Handbook for 1988/89. In the article he detailed the achievements of Tom's ministry at home and abroad, ending with the publication of a Bible Study series that was published posthumously at the 1988 Assembly entitled, "Listen to the Spirit". It was a series of Bible Studies on the letters to the seven churches in the Book of Revelation. The obituary in the Baptist Handbook spoke of the combined ministry of Tom and Doreen and of their "fine example of Christian commitment, infectious enthusiasm, missionary zeal, and brave endurance."

When the question of a Memorial to Tom and Doreen was raised, it quickly became evident that no finer tribute to the pair could be made than to press ahead with the Abbeyfield Extra Care Housing complex at Wigmore. In the January 1988 edition of the 'Tidings' David King explained the purpose of the Tom and Doreen Rogers Memorial Fund. "Each one of us, as an individual, was precious to them; each one of us has lost two irreplaceable friends. By their example they showed how husband and wife should love one another, how to bring up children, and how to reflect the love of God to others outside the family."

The Appeal went national. By July 1988 £6,000 had been raised. By January 1989 it reached £15,000. By the April that year a plot of land behind the existing Wigmore unit had been purchased. By the end of 1990 £150,000 had been raised through the Memorial Fund. The Home eventually opened in October 1992 providing care for 37 frail and elderly people. Trevor Cox had been the Project Director for Rogers House from 1988 and managed to turn the vision into a reality. He subsequently went on to be the Chief Executive of Abbeyfield, Kent. Hilary Cox (nee Shellock) was the first matron of Rogers House in 1992 and eight years later became the Society's overall Director of Care until her retirement in 2006. In the Christmas 1994 edition of the 'Tidings' David King wrote an article in which he thanked everyone who had made possible this lasting tribute to Tom and Doreen. He ended by saying "Bless you" to all those who had contributed towards the £170,000 raised for the project. (See appendix 2)

David Rogers continued his calling in the Baptist ministry. His twin brother, Mark, pursued his Christian vocation through medicine. He is currently McMillan Consultant in Clinical Genetics and Honorary Research Fellow at Cardiff and Vale University Health Board. Their sister, Pauline, eventually trained for the Anglican ministry, becoming Vicar of Wyke near Guildford. Subsequently she was appointed to Gloucester Cathedral as Diocesan Officer for Vocational Ministries and Parish Development.

CHAPTER 10

A NEW DIRECTION? CHRIS VOKE 1986 – 1996

The search for a new minister began even before Tom Rogers had concluded his ministry. In May 1985 the deacons met with Bill Hancock, the outgoing Area Superintendent. He outlined the settlement process to them. They in turn asked whether Dr Raymond Brown of Spurgeon's College might be interested in the vacant pastorate. In June the deacons decided to write to Rev Andrew Kane from Worthing and Dr Paul Beasley-Murray to ask if they would be in the frame for the pastorate. In July, somewhat exasperated by the endeavours of the deacons, Bill Hancock did suggest one name they might like to consider: Rev Christopher Voke of Upper Beeding. On the 12th September, a few days after Tom and Doreen's Farewell, the deacons met with Chris Voke after which they invited him to take services later in the year.

Chris Voke was born on 17th June 1946. He married Margaret in 1970. They had two sons, Adam (born 1974) and Zachary (born 1980). A third child, Hannah, was born in November 1985. Chris had been Travelling Secretary with UCCF from 1969 – 1972; had trained at Spurgeon's 1972 – 1976; had been at Upper Beeding since 1976, a church with 113 members; and he had served on the Spurgeon's College Council since 1980. His only hesitation in pursuing the vacancy at Gillingham was the possibility of an opening as Pastoral Studies Tutor at London Bible College.

The post at LBC did not materialise. Chris came to Green Street on Sunday 20th October 1985. He spent a couple of days looking at the various organisations, meeting with the leaders and with Tom Rogers. On 27th November he preached "with a view" after which the leaders "by a large majority" recommended the Church Meeting invite him to take up the pastorate. The Church Meeting voted 133 to 31 to invite Chris Voke to become their new minister, an 81% call. On 5th December he wrote back accepting their invitation. He was to commence his ministry on 1st April 1986 with an Induction on 12th April. Rev Jim Graham from Goldhill Baptist Church was the preacher.

In his letter of acceptance Chris Voke indicated that the words of John 15:16-17 had informed his decision and would shape his ministry. There was an evangelistic task – "to go and bear fruit, fruit that would last;" there was a vision for renewal – "then the Father will give you whatever you ask in my name;" and there was to be a new relationship between pastor and people – "This is my command, love one another."

So swift had been the settlement process that Stan Feltham from Borstal Baptist Church, who had been appointed Moderator in May 1985, had very little to do. More problematic for the church was the predicament about where Chris & Margaret Voke and the family were to live.

Back in February 1978 the Area Superintendent had written to his churches regarding the plight of Baptist Ministers in retirement. There was encouragement given to allow ministers to buy their own property wherever possible. At that time the deacons were adamant that the manse should not be sold, but the following year they changed their mind. When Tom and Doreen received a legacy they expressed the wish to buy their own property. The deacons in October 1979 suggested that the Rogers' could buy 1 Brasenose Road, and when this came to a Church Meeting on 17th October it was approved with 2 votes against and 13 abstentions. The price was set at £26,500 in the November. At this point the sale became somewhat complicated and protracted.

It was realised that the manse was covered by private trustees. In order for the Charity Commission to permit the sale of the property it was first necessary to place the house on a proper charitable foundation. Consequently, in December 1979 the Baptist Union Corporation were adopted as the trustees of the property. They in turn insisted that to avail the church the maximum amount of money, the property should be advertised locally to ascertain if there were any other interested parties. By March 1980 it transpired that only Tom and Doreen were interested in the house, and consequently the sale proceeded with completion taking place on 27th June.

The church now had no manse for a future minister. But with house prices escalating it was decided that the wisest course of action was to invest the proceeds in another property. In early 1981 the church considered properties on Kingswood Road, Cleave Road and Balmoral Road before finally purchasing 31 Gillingham Road for £30,000 in August 1981. Their intention was to use the property for single Christians and to place house-parents in overall control. It was given the name 'Rocklands'.

It soon became apparent that the purchase had been ill advised, and from the outset there were concerns about its structural soundness. Ted Andrews, the Treasurer, was so incensed when he saw the condition of the house that he felt obliged to resign as a deacon and Church Treasurer. In November a management committee was formed to oversee the house. Syd and Margaret Smith were appointed house-parents, but it became very difficult to find anyone who really wanted to live there. It rarely had more than one or two residents, and when Syd and Margaret indicated they were giving up as house-parents the church decided to sell the property. This, however, proved far from easy.

Such was the poor structural condition of the building that no bank or building society would provide a mortgage for any prospective buyers. The house was a total liability. In 1984 it was used for office space and accommodation for the team working on the "Down to Earth" Mission. For eight months it provided accommodation for a family working with Youth for Christ. But finally the only way the property could be sold was through a cash buyer. It was finally sold for £27,000 in January 1986 – that was £3,000 less than the church paid for it five years earlier!

By January 1986 the church had already been viewing properties as a possible manse and finally agreed with Chris and Margaret Voke to buy 28 Stuart Road. The property needed a lot of work doing to it, including complete rewiring. It was purchased for £42,000 and needed a further £18,000 spending on it. The house was finally ready to move into in July 1986, three months after Chris Voke had started his ministry. For most of that time his family had stayed in Upper Beeding, and Chris had commuted down lodging with a church family for part of the week. But with an overall outlay of £60,000 on the property, and only £27,000 available from the sale of Rocklands, it was agreed that the property would be bought on a 50 – 50 basis with Chris and Margaret Voke buying and owning half the house. This was to have significant implications for the church further down the road.

In September 1986 Chris Voke told the deacons that he and Margaret felt they had entered Canaan, a place of promise and expectation. In November he shared with them a vision for the future which involved "powerful worship, radical discipleship, and a more flexible organisational structure."

One of the major changes that took place in the early years of Chris' ministry was the departure of Sylvia Stevenson. Sylvia informed the deacons as early as July 1986 that she was considering looking for accreditation as a Baptist Minister, but it was July 1987 before she pursued this route and the church endorsed her candidacy. Between August and December 1987 Sylvia took a sabbatical in Louisville, Kentucky where she pursued post-graduate studies in the area of music and leading worship. In March 1988 Reg Hughes stepped down as Church Secretary, and the newly designed post of Church Administrator was filled by Sylvia. On 5th November 1988 she was ordained as a Baptist Minister after successfully passing the National Selection Conference. The service was held at Green Street. In April 1989 Sylvia informed the church that she had received a call to become minister of Tyndale Baptist Church, Reading and would be leaving Gillingham in October. Sylvia's final article for the 'Tidings' movingly mentioned her early Christian upbringing at Green Street; being baptised by Jack Pike; playing the organ while still only a teenager; her training as a teacher; her baptism in the Spirit in August 1963; her ten years in Africa; her call to ministry at Green Street; and nursing her dying mother. It had taken nine years for the pastor to be born. Sylvia said that the Bible text that had influenced her throughout her life was Zechariah 4:6 "Not by might, nor by power, but by my Spirit, says the Lord." The October 'Tidings' carried words of appreciation for Sylvia's ministry from Ted Andrews, Barbara Matthews, Hazel Mitchell, Barbara Ost and Jan Watkin. Her education classes were especially appreciated. Sylvia's Farewell Service was 29th October.

Sylvia's departure created two vacancies: the post of Church Administrator/Secretary and that of assistant minister. Short term the Administrator post was taken by Ted Andrews, but when he and Nora left the area in 1991 the role was taken on by David Howlett who had retired as Warden at the end of 1989. The post of Warden was subsequently taken on by Wolf Schulze.

To begin with not everyone in the church was convinced that a second minister was needed. But by November 1989 the consensus of opinion had changed, and it was decided that it was right to seek a second appointment. The Area Superintendent, Peter Tongemann, was consulted; a profile was drawn up of the sort of person the church were looking for; and throughout 1990 the deacons met with several people with a view to them taking on this role. In January 1991 the name of John Whitcombe of Millmead Baptist Church, Guildford, was first mentioned. John was not a Baptist Minister but the Church Administrator at Millmead. It soon became apparent, however, that his skill areas complemented those of Chris Voke. The Church Meeting in March 1991 invited John with an 85% call and John accepted this shortly afterwards.

John was married to Joan. They had three children, Andrew, Sarah and Daniel. John started at the church in September 1991 and they moved into their own property at 34 Cleave Road. John's principal area of responsibility was the pastoral care of the church, and when the Board Chairmen were revamped in 1992 John became chair of the Pastoral Board. He was subsequently to develop interest in counselling and healing ministries. John was also responsible for introducing the week by week prayer ministry in Sunday services; openness to the Holy Spirit; and the use of spiritual gifts.

Even before their arrival it was clear that Joan Whitcombe was seriously ill. Tests and in-depth medical assessment revealed that her condition would not improve and in March 1992 Joan passed away. Her death coincided with her son Andrew's baptism. The church tried to provide as much support as possible to the grieving family. Two years later, in the summer of 1994, John Whitcombe married Miv Fisher.

Another major area of change in the church came through the formation of a new Baptist Church in Walderslade. The origins of what was known as the Tunbury Avenue Fellowship started with Zion, Chatham and their mission station at Bluebell Hill. As a large housing area started to emerge in the 1970s it was deemed appropriate to try and start a new work in the vicinity. A Spurgeon's student was attached to the Bluebell Hill and Tunbury fellowships, and in January 1983 a half acre site was purchased for £2,000. By May 1983 new twinning arrangements within the KBA

Medway District had linked Gillingham Baptist Church with Tunbury, and the following year the Association Minister, Rev Michael Ridgeon, was attached to the cause.

In June 1987 Reg Hughes agreed to join the steering group which was overseeing the work at Tunbury. In March 1988 he stepped down as Church Secretary at Gillingham, and Eric Seager, on behalf of the church leaders, expressed a huge debt of gratitude to Reg for his invaluable twelve years as Church Secretary. In September 1988 the deacons said that they saw no reason why Reg could not stay on the diaconate while he was involved at Tunbury Avenue.

The Kent Baptist Association, through the local steering group, became responsible for the new church plant calling Rev Trefor Jones to the pastorate. His Induction to the newly named Walderslade Baptist Fellowship took place on the afternoon of the 5th November 1988 following an initial pastorate grant from the Baptist Union. The congregation was still meeting in a portacabin, a former Dover Harbour Board Canteen, which was far from ideal!

In 1989 the KBA churches committed themselves to try and raise the funds to erect a worship centre at Walderslade. A manse, costing £87,000 had already been purchased. When Green Street received a large legacy that year they tithed the gift and gave £3,000 to Walderslade for their new church building. By the end of 1989 Reg's involvement with Walderslade was such that he decided not to stand for re-election to the diaconate at Green Street. It was the end of 24 continuous years on the leadership at Gillingham Baptist Church.

During the first week of May 1990 the contractors, E.C. Gransden & Son, who had done the work at Green Street in 1975, moved on to the site at Catkin Close, Walderslade. The Stone Laying Ceremony was on 19th May and Rev Stan Feltham did the honours. The contract was worth £340,000. The external structure of the church building was completed by November, and the congregation were able to enter the unheated and unfinished sanctuary on Christmas Day 1990. The official opening wasn't until the 11th May 1991. Before that, on Sunday 17th March, 28 people covenanted together to become founder members of Walderslade Baptist

Church. Of these, six were from Green Street. At the Church Meeting at Green Street on 19th March 1991 Mr & Mrs M. Fleet, Mr & Mrs R. Hughes, and Mr & Mrs D. Vickery were formally transferred to the church membership of Walderslade Baptist Church, and were 'handed over' to the care of Rev Trefor Jones. In the newly formed church, Mike Fleet became Mission Secretary, David Vickery continued as Treasurer, and Reg Hughes was appointed Church Secretary. The following year Helen Vickery transferred her membership over to Walderslade. In 1996 Rev David Stedman became the minister at Walderslade. By the time he had moved to Canterbury five years later the church had 100 members.

At the same time as Walderslade was being formed a very different church planting initiative was taking place in a more familiar part of Gillingham. By the early 1980s Camden Road was running out of steam. What brought a new lease of life to the old place was the appointment of Peter Castle and Bernie Pinner to the leadership in 1985. Bernie had been heavily involved in the organisation of the 'Down to Earth' mission in 1984 and had been heading up the Youth Board at Green Street. From 1985 the reports from Camden Road became more positive and hopeful with children's work and Sunday services all taking a turn for the better. In 1986 Bernie was elected onto the Green Street diaconate. In April 1987 Bernie's article in the 'Tidings' highlighted the fairly dilapidated condition of the old building: "A recent survey has showed that the floor is bowing and the walls are falling out. A lot of money will be required for repairs and the question of rebuilding must be faced. Perhaps this would mean a new site in Lower Gillingham." In December he produced another stark assessment of the state of the Mission Hall: "Already we have leaks in the roof causing damage to the main hall, kitchen, back room and hall. Something needs to be done to preserve the poor state of the building." The question was, should they rebuild or should they repair?

Through a series of prayer meetings at Green Street and Camden Road during 1987 a vision began to emerge which was articulated in February 1988 as the need to build and equip God's people in two congregations. Chris Voke, in all his public statements, was clear that Camden Road was a potential growth area and that time and money should be invested to help realise that potential. As the year progressed there was a growing conviction that the Mission Hall should be rebuilt on the same site. A

Camden Road Building Fund was established. During the year an extensive programme of visitation around Camden Road was carried out. It was known as 'Contact 88'. At the end of 1988 Bernie Pinner and Ron Smith were both elected as elders at Green Street.

In 1989 initial plans for a new building were drawn up. The Building Fund was given a real boost when Green Street received a legacy of £29,572 from Mrs Goodwin of Dawes Street. This was half the proceeds of the sale of her house. £3,000 was given to Walderslade for their new building; the remainder went to Camden Road. In 1990 a set of plans were submitted for planning approval to Gillingham Borough Council but were turned down ostensibly because of a lack of car parking provision.

The congregational life at Camden Road was going from strength to strength. Bernie Pinner wrote in the 'Tidings' for January 1991 that the average Sunday morning congregation was between 50 and 60 people. The previous Family Service, which had been led by Chris Voke, had seen well over 90 people in attendance. A snapshot of the strength of the Green Street congregation at this time can be gauged by a Congregation Count taken on 15th October 1989 when it was reported that there were 151 people present at the Sunday morning service and 129 people present at the evening service.

David Hibbin, a student from Spurgeon's College, was linked with Camden Road, and he and his wife, Sue, were providing regular ministry. During 1990 the Mission had resumed its own Evening Services again after many years. In 1991 the Mission celebrated its 70th Anniversary. In November 1991 a document was produced entitled "Steps Towards Independence". It looked at forming a separate Membership Roll for Camden Road; responsibility for its own running costs and finance; and its own leadership by May 1992. The document proved a little hopeful. Leadership elections at Camden Road didn't take place until January 1993 when Roger Barrett was elected to join Bernie. In June 1993 Clive Waters and John Lownds were also elected. In 1994 a considerable amount of improvement was carried out to the shell of the old Mission Hall building in the hope that it would last for a few more years. An application was made to Baptist Home Mission for an initial pastorate grant, although finances were reported as sufficiently healthy that they could support a minister even without Home Mission support.

Finally, at a Green Street Church Meeting on Tuesday 20th September 1994 some 57 members from Green Street were formally transferred to Camden Road Baptist Fellowship. On Sunday 25th September there was a Service of Dedication led by Peter Tongemann, the Area Superintendent. On Wednesday 28th the inaugural Church Meeting of the Camden Road Baptist Fellowship took place.

One of the other tasks carried out in 1994 was to obtain permission from the Charity Commission and the Baptist Union to use the Camden Road Building Fund money, if need be, to buy a manse. This turned out to be a fortuitous move. The church's quest for a minister did not prove easy. Chris Voke moderated for a period of time before Reg Hughes took over. It wasn't until February 1998 that Rev Darren Blaney accepted a call to be the minister at Camden Road at the same time as the church made a decision to purchase the Bridge House pub on the corner of Bridge Road and Medway Road. Darren and Erica Blaney and their four children moved into Bridge House much to the mirth of the local papers: "The vicar's home will be a pub" headlined the Kent Messenger's free paper on Friday 27th February. "Holy Spirit in large measures" ran the 'Medway News'. Darren remained minister at 'The Bridge', as it became known, until 2006 when he moved to Herne Bay. When the Camden Road building was finally condemned the congregation moved into the Sunlight Centre on Richmond Road and continued to serve that part of Lower Gillingham but this time from a new community facility and a new location.

The effect of losing 57 members to Camden Road at the same time as losing 7 members to Walderslade was quite depressing for the mother church. Church membership which had stood at 428 at the end of 1984 was down to 229 by the end of 1994. Not surprisingly, therefore, when Rev Colin Buchanan from St Mark's began to talk with the leaders at Green Street in 1995 about becoming involved in an exciting new church planting initiative on St Mary's Island the response was not favourable. The Church Meeting in July of that year made it abundantly clear that they had had their fill of helping to plant new causes, and the church leadership were sent a clear message from the floor of the meeting. There was more interest in providing support for Twydall Baptist Church which at this time was at a very low ebb. In December 1995 church membership at Green Street stood at 209.

While attention was focussed on the developments at Camden Road, there were also plenty of dreams about what could be done at Green Street. In 1992 a 'Vision for Green Street' document identified several ambitious ideas:

"We will redesign and rebuild the lower front entrances of the church to make one clear entrance and hallway with reception and improved security. This will create a more inviting access to the church with a view into the reception and coffee shop area." It concluded with a wish to "Refurbish the inside of the church; remove pews and install chairs downstairs; refit the pulpit area to make the church more adaptable to the kind of worship and teaching we envisage."

Hazel Mitchell had been a passionate advocate of developing a regular coffee shop. She saw this as having a great missionary purpose. Margaret Howlett was to run the Wednesday morning coffee shop while Joyce Black and Val Hopkins ran it on Saturday morning.

The separation of Camden Road was to make a huge dint in the leadership at Green Street. With Bernie Pinner, Jean Millgate and Mark Johnson going over to the new cause, and Hazel Mitchell stepping down, there was a desperate need for new blood to replenish the church leadership. At the end of 1992 Lillian Smith stepped down as Church Treasurer and was replaced by Lyn Newlan. David Howlett had picked up the role of Church Secretary in March 1991. He had tried to relinquish the post at the end of 1992 but was persuaded to stay on for a further fifteen months. In January 1994 the church agreed to appoint Lyn Newlan as both Church Secretary and Church Treasurer. While a number of people would have preferred to have two people for two posts, in point of fact there was plenty of precedent for the two roles being held by the same person. Both Mr Dyke and Mr Winfield had done so to great effect in previous generations. In November 1995 Paul Bishop, Anne Newnham and Rachel Pemberton were elected to the diaconate for the first time. In July 1996 Steve Barber was elected an elder.

The church's missionary interest remained as strong as ever. In December 1986 Joe and Rachel Davis shared with the church their sense of calling into full time Christian ministry. In July 1987 they joined Oasis with Steve Chalke and began working at Mitcham Lane Baptist Church, Streatham. In 1989 they went to Spurgeon's College and trained on the Evangelism and Church Planting course. Joe was ordained at West Croydon Baptist Church in July 1997. In 1987 Ros Wilkes shared with the church her interest in Christian service. In 1990 she moved to Catshill, Bromsgrove and from there went to train at Regents Park College, Oxford since when she has served churches in the North East and the East Midlands. In 1989 Miv Fisher went on a training programme with YWAM which took her as far as Marseilles. Bill Clark joined Green Street in 1989. In 1991 he began investigating full time youth work training. Two years later the church approved his application to join Moorlands Bible College. In 1994 Bill shared with the church his vision for a youth 'drop-in' facility on Gillingham High Street, and in April he was part of the inaugural planning meeting for a Gillingham Youth Centre.

In 1994 the church sent Chris and Margaret Voke out to Nairobi to visit Russ and Lyn Noble. At the same time Eric and Margaret Seager went out to Lebanon to support partners in mission in that beleaguered community. For a number of years a twinning arrangement was maintained with Rouen Baptist Church. Chris Voke, Liz Rowland, Eric Seager and Roy Jones made several visits to Rouen and took part in various evangelistic events. Younger members of the church were also expressing their interest in mission. In 1992 Carolyn Hughes went out to Jamaica for a year with the BMS. In 1995 Ruth Newnham went out to Japan, and in 1996 Sarah Jones went out to India with Operation Mobilisation. The following year Roy Jones went out to serve as a doctor in Nigeria. In 1996 all the Gillingham Baptist Churches joined forces to support their new BMS link missionary, Dr Simon Collins, who was about to go out to Angola. Before his departure he married Karen Hedge at Sittingbourne Baptist Church on 20th April.

The church's generosity towards mission continued to be hugely impressive. In 1991 the church gave £33,784 to mission. In 1995 they gave

123

£42,659 out of an annual income of £124,552. Much of this went to support those individuals the church had commissioned, as well as to organisations with which the church had close ties.

The church continued to be very energetic in the area of evangelism. In 1989 the Billy Graham Livelink proved a great success. Some 489 people went forward at the Chatham venue, 20 of whom were referred to Gillingham Baptist Church for follow up. In 1991 Anne Newnham ran a very successful Holiday Club for children. The King's Club saw 84 children at the church over the week and paved the way for similar clubs over the next few years. In 1991 the Gillingham 'March for Jesus' also took place. Hazel Mitchell continued to organise the "Teach and Reach" evangelistic programme, formerly Evangelism Explosion. Jane Jones was involved in the 'On Fire' evangelistic programme across Medway in 1994 and 1995. This involved Open Air events at The Strand as well as visits to various schools. In 1995 Chris Voke also started the first Alpha Course at the church. By 1996 this had become very successful with seven conversions reported, and it was to serve as an invaluable tool for evangelism and discipleship over the next twenty years.

Changes were taking place to the worship style in the church. In 1994 the first of two tailor-made song books was produced for congregational use. Many people in the church were refreshed through annual visits to Spring Harvest in Minehead. Church family life was also strengthened through a number of church holidays organised by Jenny Matthias. Behind the scenes there was lots of quiet and patient work being carried out. On Sunday evenings, for example, Arthur and Joan Johnson hosted an after church Young People's Fellowship which proved very popular.

Lyn Newlan's vestry report for 1996 looked back on the previous year's main events.

"There has been considerable emphasis on the Holy Spirit during the year, and in March the elders and deacons met with Roger Mitchell and a team from the Ichthus Fellowship to pray and seek God regarding the move of the Spirit that appeared to be affecting so many churches ..... some people have been greatly blessed but others have struggled with some of the changes that have taken place."

In May 1994 Chris Voke spoke to the deacons about the possibility of buying 28 Stuart Road outright. The original arrangement back in 1986 permitted this option, and Chris and Margaret were now in a position to act on this. The manse was subsequently valued at £75,000, and in March 1995 permission was granted by the Charity Commission for the sale to proceed. The Accounts for the year 1995 had an item entitled 'Manse Fund' and alongside this heading was the sum £37,970 which was the church's 50% from the sale.

On 24th March 1996 Chris Voke wrote a letter of resignation to the church. He had been invited to become a tutor at Spurgeon's College with special responsibility for the church-based pastoral students. He would be part of the Applied Theology team. Chris had enjoyed a three month sabbatical in the autumn of 1992 during which time he had made a study of Biblical prophecy with particular relation to the Book of Zechariah. Now he was able to pursue further his own theological studies at the same time as training others for the ministry. In his letter for the 'Tidings' in summer 1996 he expressed his thanks for the love that he and Margaret had been shown over the ten years they had been part of the fellowship.

On Saturday 29th June there was a Farewell Concert at the church with Derek Winn serving as compere. The following day, Chris and Margaret Voke served communion to the whole church as their parting act.

The procedure for knowing what to do next was more complex than it had ever been before. The church already had a minister, John Whitcombe, and some felt that he should be offered the senior post. Others were mindful that John was not an accredited Baptist Minister. Still others felt that John should also resign and clear the way for a new appointment. Concerns over finance were a factor in this. Covering the cost of two ministers as well as those serving as missionaries was an increasing struggle for a shrinking membership. In the end, the leaders affirmed John Whitcombe in his ministry, and a decision to search for a senior minister was postponed until November.

The Church Meeting on 19th November 1996 had 91 members present. Steve Barber opened in worship and the chair was taken by David Taylor, the new Area Superintendent. Feelings were running high and were not helped by some overly strict chairmanship. The outcome of the meeting, however, was an overwhelming decision to start the process of searching for a new senior minister to head up the leadership team.

During 1996 the church saw the closure of the Playgroup which had been such a part of the life of the church for many years. The church was also obliged to remove the iconic pinnacles from the front of the church building. These had become unstable, and David Holloway, the chair of the Fabric Board, organised their safe removal. During 1997 the King's Club, which had met on Wednesday evenings for a number of years, closed down. The church also had to work through the implications of the new Disability Discrimination Act. Various adaptations were made to the building, and in January 1998 a new Disabled Toilet was completed. The Children's Act also required the church to implement new policies and practices with regard to safeguarding the welfare of children in their care.

The Pastoral Vacancy in 1997 saw a number of high profile speakers at Green Street including Roy Crowne the National Director of Youth for Christ; Faith Forster and Roger Mitchell from Ichthus; Darrell Jackson from the Baptist Union; Norman Moss and Rob Warner from Queens Road, Wimbledon; and Jeff Lucas. There was also an evening celebration in March 1998 led by Noel Richards, one of the country's leading worship leaders.

In the summer of 1998 John Whitcombe made a visit to Uganda as part of his sabbatical leave. He tied this in with a visit to Lyn and Russ Noble. Later in the year John and Miv went to Chicago where they spent time learning about the Willow Creek model of ministry.

CHAPTER 11

PUTTING THE HOUSE IN ORDER: DAVE JOHN 1998 – 2007

The original profile for a new minister, drawn up by the eldership, caused a major problem. The document specified that the church was looking for a man. Arguments as to why leadership in the church should be male were presented to the church in January 1997, but there was clearly some vocal opposition. The argument carried on through the first few months of the year and became quite heated. Finally on 15th April a Church Meeting was called to settle the matter. Michael Fanstone, from Gravesend Baptist Church, was brought in to chair the meeting, and when it was put to the vote there were 39 votes in favour of specifying that the senior minister had to be male while 44 were prepared to accept a male or female senior minister. The church profile was amended accordingly.

During 1997 the church explored two possible candidates for the senior minister role but neither of these came to anything. Finally from the December list, the leaders agreed to meet with Rev David John who was the associate minister at Battle Baptist Church near Hastings. Dave came to meet the leaders on 5th January, preached on 25th January, and preached 'with a view' on 22rd February. The Church Meeting on Tuesday 24th February 1998 was chaired by Steve Barber and resulted in Dave John being invited to the pastorate by a vote of 103 to 2. Lyn Newlan rang Dave during the meeting to inform him of the vote, and by the end of the evening he had accepted.

Once again there was the issue of where to live. The church agreed that any new property obtained had to be on the same 50-50 arrangement they had originally with Chris and Margaret Voke. On this basis a house at 78 Malvern Road was purchased, completion taking place at the end of July 1998. Dave's Induction took place on Sunday 20th September at 3.30pm. The preacher was Rev Dennis Nolan, the pastor of Battle Baptist Church.

Soon after Dave and Alison John moved into the house on Malvern Road, along with their children Katy, Debbie and Gareth, they were made aware of a potential major problem. At the Leaders Meeting in September 1998 mention was made of the fact that no planning consent had been obtained by the previous owners of 78 Malvern Road for the loft conversion. By December Medway Council had written to the church informing them they were taking out an enforcement order to have the dormer windows at the rear of the house removed. The changes the council were asking for would involve the church in major expense and would significantly reduce the size of some of the upstairs rooms. The church provided assurances that no such issues had been flagged up at the time of the purchase, and in the end, mercifully, the matter was dropped.

Both Dave and Alison brought strong musical gifts to this ministry. They developed worship teams in the coming years with a rota of musicians and singers. Dave would play and sing for the toddler group, Steps. Alison was involved in several major musical productions including 'Rumours of Angels' in 1999, and 'Hopes and Dreams' in 2000 which was run in conjunction with St Marks. Dave often used his puppet, Arnie, in the all-age part of services. Both he and Alison participated as chaplains to the various Brigade camps at Downton, near Salisbury, where a number of first time Christian commitments were made. Dave was keen to develop a collaborative style of decision making and to develop the gifts of local leaders. It is noticeable that the chairmanship of Leaders Meetings and Church Meetings was frequently taken by other members of the leadership team.

Back in 1997 Lyn Newlan had made it plain that she did not wish to continue as Treasurer past the next AGM. By the end of that year Margaret Seager had agreed to take on that role and she was duly appointed by the church at the beginning of 1998. In December 1998 Margaret shared with the leaders her strong conviction that Alison John's gifts should be recognised by the church. Alison was playing a major role in the leading of worship, and clearly had a vision for working with women in the life of the fellowship. Margaret felt very strongly that Alison should be paid for the work she was doing. In March 1999 Margaret presented this same belief to the Church Meeting with a recommendation that Alison should receive £3,000 a year. The meeting had plenty of views on this subject but finally agreed with the recommendation. The same meeting also agreed that Bill Clark should be supported as a missionary to young people in Gillingham. He was planning to reduce his hours with Customs & Excise to make room for this work with local youngsters. It was a long meeting which finally ended at 10.45pm!

It was interesting that the Church Meeting in March 2000 unanimously reaffirmed Alison's appointment with no discussion whatsoever. There was clearly deep appreciation of the contribution she was making to the life of the church. She and Miv Whitcombe had been running Ladies' Discipleship groups and pastoral groups during the day. But one of the other major changes they introduced at this time was the transition of the Women's Meeting, which Mildred Collings had been leading, into Prime Time, an afternoon service for men and women from a much wider age range. Meeting on a fortnightly and then a weekly basis, Prime Time attracted between 35 and 40 people providing opportunities for teaching, prayer and fellowship.

Margaret Seager's tenure as Treasurer was to be a brief one. In 1997 both Eric Seager and Steve Barber started training at Spurgeon's College. Steve stepped down from the eldership soon after this to concentrate on his ministerial training and church placement responsibilities. Eric had not originally seen training as a route into Baptist ministry, but in 1998 the church and the College approved his transfer to the ministerial programme and accreditation. In November 1999, still with nine months of his course to complete, Eric received a call to become minister of Harston Baptist Church near Cambridge. His acceptance of that invitation meant that Margaret also had to relinquish her role as Treasurer of Gillingham Baptist Church.

In January 2000 Chris Barr was appointed Church Treasurer. The same meeting also appointed Bill Clark as an elder. Bill's appointment was all the more important because of the imminent departure of Eric Seager, the only remaining elder. In March 2000 Steve Barber accepted a call to become minister of Minster Road, Sheppey. The summer saw a joint Ordination Service at Green Street for Eric and Steve as they prepared to move off to their respective ministries. There was a deep expression of appreciation for both men. Eric Seager, in particular, had been in church leadership at Green Street for 25 years.

In March 2000 Chris Barr became seriously unwell, and by the July he had to tender his resignation. With oversight of the church finances in some turmoil Lyn Newlan agreed to take over as Treasurer once again. But it soon became plain that the church was heading for a major financial crisis.

At the end of 1998 Margaret Seager had warned the leaders that the church was approaching a financial cliff edge. Income for that year had been £14,500 below the budget. This hadn't been too disastrous because of the £15,500 surplus built up during 1997 when the church was without a senior minister. The Church Meeting in November 1998 approved a 3% pay increase for the staff for the coming year.

Twelve months later things were no better. Margaret Seager informed the Church Meeting in November 1999 that the church was facing a £19,000 deficit on the year. The only thing that was saving them this time from disaster was an anonymous and one-off gift of £10,000, and an interim payment of £4,000 from the estate of the late Shirley Wenham. The November Church Meeting approved a 2% pay increase for the staff.

At the start of the year 2000 there were six members of staff on the pay roll. Dave John was senior minister; John Whitcombe was associate minister; Alison John was the very part time appointment; Mo Purser was clerical assistant, a position she had held for the past 13 years; and Stan Brown was the full time caretaker. At the Leaders Meeting in July 2000 Lyn Newlan presented the team with a stark warning. They were heading for a deficit by the end of the year of £32,600. Salaries, which had formed 50% of the overall budget in 1980, had consumed 87% of the budget in 1999. This was wholly unsustainable especially since there was pressing and expensive work needed to be done to the church building. The options before them were limited. They could use the £21,000 from Shirley Wenham's legacy, but this would only put off painful decisions for a little longer, or they could look to reduce all outgoings by 23%. Lyn told the Church Meeting that the church was changing. There were fewer large earners; they had lost a number of regular givers; and all this had an impact on the Gift Aid money. The word that she felt had come from the Lord was a need "to put our house in order." The church needed to be good stewards of the things God had entrusted to them.

In July 2000 Mo Purser informed the church that she had found a new job and would be leaving at the end of the summer. A decision was made to look for voluntary help to staff the church office. In September Alison John made it plain that she was willing to forego her salary. Still, the leadership team meeting that month had to face some very difficult decisions, and the outcome was a recommendation to terminate the employment of the caretaker, and the employment of John Whitcombe.

On Tuesday 17th October a Special Church Meeting was called. It was chaired by Steve Barber. The Meeting was very awkward. John and Miv Whitcombe did not feel that their ministry at Green Street was over, and a number of members spoke in their defence. John felt aggrieved at the way decisions had been made. But in the end, faced with the impending financial precipice, the Meeting reluctantly agreed to the redundancies. A Farewell Bring and Share lunch was held for John and Miv on Sunday 17th December.

In January 2001 a handful of members resigned over the way John had been treated. By May 2001 John and Miv were actively involved in King's Church, Chatham and felt it was right to transfer their membership as well. Time was to prove something of a healer. When John Whitcombe passed away in 2007, Miv asked for the service to take place at Gillingham Baptist Church. It was conducted by Chris Voke.

The year 2000 had not been altogether disastrous. In June, Bernie and Chris Pinner, back from Camden Road, were released to take on leadership roles at St Mary's Island Church. In the July, Jenny Boucher shared with the church her vision for a ladies' social craft group which she had seen work well as an evangelistic tool in Australia. The church agreed to run with the experiment. In September, the church also agreed a new Mission Statement: to "Build God's Community in the heart of Gillingham" and continued to work through a series of Core Values. In November, the Mission Board approved Mark and Sarah Newnham's overseas missionary service. Remarkably, in spite of all the financial woes, the church membership for the year saw an increase from 224 to 231 members.

Ecumenical collaboration throughout this period was also strong. 'Medway Celebrate' saw nationally acclaimed worship leaders Paul Oakley and Noel

Richards visit the towns. 'Compassion for Kent' in 1999 saw a visit from Ed Silvoso and a team from Argentina. Dave John was subsequently to make his own visit to Argentina at the end of 1999. 'Priestfield 2000' saw the football stadium used for a joint churches evangelistic event. There was also a close partnership with Gillingham Youth for Christ which saw Green Street members accommodating members of the GYFC team as well as helping out at the 'shop' drop-in. In August 2000 the church eagerly supported the New Wine type festival on the Detling Showground. Called 'Revival Fire' it subsequently became an annual event and went on to be a great encouragement and inspiration to large numbers of people. Several people from Green Street helped out at Detling. Vera Paley was particularly valued for her work with the young people.

In 2000 a Premises Working Group was set up chaired by Bill Clark. The group was given the remit of looking imaginatively at the overall future of the buildings. Their report in September made clear they had looked at various radical options including moving to another location and constructing purpose-built premises. In the end they felt that financial constraints and lack of adequate alternative accommodation meant that a refurbishment of the present buildings was the best option. The Report concluded: "The next stage in the Project will be to identify the areas of the building which would need developing to facilitate the desired purposes and mission of the church."

By 2002 it had become clear that the area of the building that was ripe for redevelopment was the coffee shop area. Access into and out of this area had long been an issue with steep steps descending down from the entrance. Thoughts about stair lifts were considered until the idea of raising the actual floor level was raised by Colin Stutton, and found to be the most sensible way forward. The original budget for the scheme had been £17,000 but this had risen to £30,000 by the middle of the year. By June 2002 the church had £22,000 in a Project Fund with the hope of receiving a portion of the sale of the old Baptist Church buildings at Zion, Chatham which had recently closed. In the end, £7,500 came from that source. Work began on the refurbishment in August 2002. The old back yard of the church was enclosed and utilised as a storage area and new cupboards were fixed into the rear of the church hall. The room that had acted as the crèche was turned into a servery linking the kitchen with the coffee shop. The work was completed in January 2003 and officially opened in the Easter. A competition was held to find the most suitable name for the new space. 'The Haven', 'The Lounge', and 'The Lighthouse' were the finalists with 'The Lighthouse' attracting most votes. In May 2003 Lyn Newlan informed the church that the overall cost of the project had been in excess of £46,000.

In the summer of 2002 Dave and Alison John celebrated their silver wedding anniversary. A special meal was prepared for them by Dorothy Marshall. Later that same year Dave and Alison took some sabbatical leave. Dave's theme was "Preaching in Contemporary Society" and explored issues of communication in 21st century culture.

With the major building project completed at church, attention returned again to staffing issues. In January 2002 Fred Adams was appointed Administrator, working two mornings a week. His hours were increased later that same year. In June 2003 Bill Clark raised the issue of taking on another staff member to deal with ministry issues. The Finance Team looked at the possibilities and reported back to the leadership that the church could afford either a part time member of staff or a student pastor. Income was running at between £1,000 and £1,500 a month over budget. Consequently, at the November 2003 Church Meeting, a secret ballot on whether to pursue a second paid member of the Ministry Team received 100% approval from those present.

Linda Smith from Spurgeons College had shared with the church leaders how a student placement would work. In March 2004 the profile of Billy Gilvear was received from the college. Billy had an army background and his dramatic conversion has since been told in his autobiography 'Storming Home'[1]. He came to preach at Green Street in April, and at a Special Church Meeting held on 4th May it was agreed (39 votes to 7) to invite Billy to come as student pastor. His induction took place on Sunday 26th September.

The problem over accommodation was helped in no small measure by the decision of Dave and Alison John to take up the option of purchasing the remaining 50% of 78 Malvern Road. They had considered this in 2002 but had not taken it any further. But in January 2004 the Church Meeting gave permission for the sale to proceed, and from the sale in September the church received £95,000.

Short term the church rented 53 St Mary's Road for Billy & Bev Gilvear and their children Jordan, Jack, Ben and then Lydia. It borrowed £25,000 from the KBA and used £15,000 of church reserves in order to have sufficient capital to buy a manse outright. A property on Rosebery Road was looked at along with one on Toronto Road, but in the end the church purchased 56 Kingswood Road for £132,000. Completion was in January 2005 and the Gilvears moved in during February.

Billy's involvement at the church was limited because of the heavy responsibilities he had with college work. But he did help with Alpha courses, one of which was held at Brompton Barracks. In 2005 he helped the church work through a mission strategy based on the 'Sowing, Reaping, Keeping' model. Billy's preaching could be challenging, and it took some people a while to adjust to his strong Scottish accent! When he began to struggle with various health issues later in 2005 and suspended his time at the College, the church kept faith with Billy and allowed him to continue his work within the fellowship.

The church mission budget during this period was reaching record levels. During 1999 the church donated over £51,000 to missionary causes and missionary personnel. By 2003 the church had separated the mission support work into an Away Board and a Home Board. That year they donated £36,000 to overseas mission and £8,000 to missionary work locally. Bill Clark's newly formed organisation, Word on the Street, received charitable status in March 2002 for its work with disadvantaged young people. He was accredited by the Baptist Union as a Youth Specialist in April 2002, and received ordination in March 2004. Norman Tharby, one of the Regional Ministers, conducted the service. Mark and Sarah Newnham took time to discern where God might be calling them, and in September 2002 they received their official farewell from the church as they prepared to move out with Mission Aviation Fellowship to Africa. Twelve months later Roy and Jane Jones, Sarah's parents, were also commissioned as they went out to do medical work in Chad with Mission Africa.

In September 2004 Alison John, Lyn Newlan and Bernie Pinner started a Lay Preachers Course at Spurgeon's. In February 2005 Alison John shared with the leaders her sense of calling to Baptist ministry. By 2006 this had been refined, and the Church Meeting in March endorsed her accreditation with the Baptist Union as an evangelist, with special focus on older people. Her placement was with the Abbeyfield Kent Society, and her work there was commended to the meeting by Trevor Cox who was Chief Executive of the Society.

A snapshot of the strength of the church at this time can be gauged from the annual Congregation Counts which the Baptist Union requested. On the 2nd December 2001 there were 116 members present at church and 169 non-members. That gave a total of 285 people at this Parade Service. Of these 87 were under 14, and 27 were aged between 14 and 21. At a Leaders Meeting in April 2004 it was reported that the evening service, which had been brought down into the Lighthouse, was now at full capacity. Other mid week groups such as Prime Time and Steps (the toddler group run by Liz Clark) were also reporting record attendances.

The church was changing too. Hazel Mitchell's Annual Report in February 2003 referred to the changing cultural mix of the fellowship, with people from all over the world joining the church. New members came into the church with backgrounds from Africa, the Caribbean, South America, and the Indian sub-continent. The changing cultural diversity within Gillingham was being felt in the worshipping life of the Baptist Church as well. Simon and Karen Collins, who had joined the church after their time with BMS, took a leading role in this move to increasing inclusivity.

But for all these exciting and encouraging signs, there were some problems that would not go away. One of these was the low attendance at Church Meetings. This was nothing new, and had been a problem that had dogged previous ministries. But for ten years it became an acute issue. In July 1999, November 2000, and July 2001 Church Meetings were not quorate. In 2002 four Church Meetings failed to attract sufficient members to officially transact business. In May and July 2003 Meetings were not quorate, and again in February and May 2006. The AGM in 2007, chaired by Billy Gilvear, did not have a quorum, and the same problem re-occurred in February 2008 and May 2009.

Another persistent problem resurfaced in March 2002 when Lyn Newlan and Rachel Pemberton failed to get elected onto the eldership. Both of them had been elected deacons in the previous November along with Alison John and Lorraine Schulze, but eldership was becoming a thorny issue once again. This was particularly frustrating for some people in the church. Dave John had spent a considerable amount of time teaching about the respective roles of elders and deacons, and had strongly endorsed the candidacy of women elders. Tensions over women in leadership continued to be an issue until finally Lyn and Rachel were both elected as elders in 2006 along with Bill Clark and Simon Collins.

Church membership numbers also started to take a dip after encouraging beginnings. A small rise in membership during 1998, 1999 and 2000 was followed by a steady period of decline so that the membership which had stood at 231 at the end of 2000 stood at 179 by the end of 2007. Some longstanding members had moved away: Val Hopkins to Rochester (2003); Doreen Barnes to Sheringham (2004); David King to Maidstone (2004); David & Dorothy Marshall (2004); Steve & Jenny Boucher to Australia in 2006; John & Liz Thompson to Spain in 2008. The period also saw the loss of some key members through death: Brian Smithson (2002); Ivy Weller, Betha Dettmer and Andy East (2003); Jenny Matthias (2006).

Other significant changes were also taking place. In 1999 the 'Tidings' finally came to an end. It had been produced as a quarterly magazine for several years but had now finally run its course, thus breaking a link going back to the 1920s. In 2004 John Buckley concluded his second period of service on the diaconate having made a major contribution to the maintenance and improvement of the buildings. That same year also saw Hilary Cox take on the oversight of the pastoral care co-ordinators in the church. Hazel Mitchell finally resigned from church leadership in 2006. She had served as Church Secretary between 2001 and 2004, and prior to that had held a series of high profile positions in the church and the Association. Trevor Purser also completed his period of service on the diaconate after over twenty years. There was huge appreciation for the work he had accomplished over that time. Rob Phipps took on the role of

Church Treasurer at the beginning of 2006 but felt the need to relinquish the role towards the end of the year, with Lyn Newlan again taking up the position.

In 2005 the church worked through the 'Purpose Driven life' course which a number of people found very beneficial. In the August Dave John began studying for a Masters Degree at Spurgeon's. At the end of 2005 the church formally joined the newly formed South East Baptist Association after several years of wrangling between the various older Associations in the South Eastern Area.

In September 2006 Dave John informed the Church Meeting of his call to Durrington New Life Church in Worthing. He and Alison had their Farewell weekend on the 13th/14th January 2007. The Saturday evening was a ceilidh held in St Mark's Church. Alison was to retain longer links with Gillingham through her placement with Abbeyfield. In 2009 she returned to Green Street for her ordination as a Baptist Minister.

Billy Gilvear continued his training at Green Street during 2007. He chaired the AGM in March that year. His final Sunday at Gillingham was 15th July before Billy, Bev and the children moved off to Guernsey. Billy had received a call as assistant minister with responsibility for evangelism at Shiloh Baptist Church. His penultimate sermon at Green Street was based on Ezekiel 37, "Son of Man, can these bones live?" His final sermon was based on 1 Corinthians chapter 13 and the pre-eminence of love. Billy is currently working as an evangelist with 'The Message' in Manchester.

The Pastoral Vacancy that followed proved to be far longer than anyone could have expected. For whatever reasons, candidates for the Vacancy simply did not work out. In 2009 Rev Mike Stanbrook was invited to act as a paid Moderator, and he helped to steer the church through some important decisions.

Although an unsettling period, the Pastoral Vacancy did achieve some important outcomes. One of these was the redevelopment of the whole church kitchen. Plans for this had been mentioned as far back as 2006, but in May 2007 a Kitchen Planning Team met with an architect and engineer to look at what could be done. The original plan was very ambitious and in

September 2008 the kitchen budget was set at £63,519. This would have involved major structural alterations and would only have been possible if a £50,000 grant from Biffa, the waste management company, had been successful. When this was turned down in May 2009 a revised plan was drawn up. The new kitchen, costing £30,000, was up and running by March 2010. Money accrued from general fund surpluses made the project possible.

The church also successfully managed to sell the old manse during the Vacancy. Once the Gilvears had moved out of 56 Kingswood Road it was decided to allow the missionary families to use the property while on furlough. In October 2007 it was decorated and repaired in advance of Mark and Sarah Newnham moving in, while in 2009 Roy and Jane Jones occupied the property before they returned to Chad. In 2010 the house was put up for sale, and once a buyer was found the completion took place at the end of July. The house sold for £144, 600. A small group was set the task of searching for a new manse, and in October 2010 a property at 5 Seaton Road was identified as meeting their requirements. The house sale went through by the end of the year at a cost of £181,000.

The church was able to make up the difference between selling the one house and buying another through a legacy they had received from the late May Langford. May's husband, Frank, had died back in 1989. He had been a veteran of World War 1 and a member of Green Street since 1920. Frank Langford ("Uncle Frank") had taught himself New Testament Greek and used his knowledge not only to enhance his own lay preaching but to help upwards of 70 men and women, many of whom went on to theological colleges or Christian ministry. Frank's lifelong commitment to serve the church of Jesus Christ was aptly remembered by this Langford Legacy. The church at Green Street tithed the gift, and with it allowed the Mission Aviation Fellowship (MAF) to construct an aircraft hangar in Kampala.

During 2010 and early 2011 there was also major expenditure on the outside of the building with repairs to crumbling stone work, and major alterations to the worship area. The platform at the front of the sanctuary was lowered to baptistery level, and there was a major investment in the visual equipment in church. A new projector was installed along with new monitors, all of which made a major improvement to the technical performance on Sundays.

Perhaps one of the most important advances the church made through the Pastoral Vacancy was the adoption of a new Church Constitution. Reference to making changes to the constitution appeared as far back as April 2005, but it wasn't until July 2009 that a Constitution Working Group was set up with Lyn Newlan, Hilary Cox and Alun Wintle making up the membership of the group. The September Church Meeting that year adopted the first proposal from the Working Group, namely the reduction of the quorum needed at church meetings from 20% of the membership to 15%. In a stroke this addressed one of the biggest problems that had dogged the church for the previous 40 years.

In March 2010 Lyn Newlan introduced to the Church Meeting various options regarding the membership of the church. The nub of the issue was whether to remain as a Closed Membership church with associate members, or whether to become an Open Membership church allowing those who had not received believers' baptism to become full members. The discussion continued at the April Church Meeting and was finally resolved at the Special Church Meeting on 18th May 2010. With 59 members at the meeting it was decided by 72% of those present and voting to become an Open Membership church. This was above the two-thirds threshold required by the constitution. Consequently, as part of the meeting, Lyn was able to welcome the former associate members into full church membership. This put right an anomaly that had existed in the church virtually since its founding back in 1879.

At the Church Meeting on 16th November 2010 it was finally agreed to the adoption of a whole new Church Constitution based on the Baptist Union's new Model Trust. There were no votes against or abstentions.

In spite of making these huge advances through the Pastoral Vacancy the fact remains it proved a very difficult time for the church. Several families moved away to join other churches; other people left the district altogether. Evening services were reduced to once a month because of the difficulty in getting people to lead them or to attend. In the end the evening services were closed. Church membership which stood at 179 in

139

2007 had fallen to 164 by November 2010, but even this figure was to prove inaccurate. In 2011 the Pastoral Team identified nearly 40 non-attending church members. On 13th September 2009 an official Congregation Count requested by the Baptist Union recorded only 78 adults and 20 children present at the morning service. The following year the Baptist Union asked for average attendance figures and those submitted reported 60 adults and 30 children. To improve the experience on Sunday mornings the balcony was closed in 2010 to ensure everyone sat in the main body of the worship area. The May 2010 Church Meeting spoke of a crisis in the Sunday School. There was such a shortage of teachers that consideration was given to conducting all-age services every week.

The burdens on the church leaders were also pressing. At the start of the Pastoral Vacancy there had been four elders. By the end only Bill Clark and Lyn Newlan remained, and Bill felt the need to step down during 2011. There had been resignations and departures from the diaconate as well, although additions in November 2009 and again in November 2010 brought the number nearly up to full strength.

In August 2010 Rev Stephen Greasley came to meet the leadership team. He preached in the October and was invited to preach 'with a view' on 28th November. Stephen had held pastorates in Matson, Gloucester (1988 - 1998) and Pear Tree, Derby (from 1998). He had been married to Sharon for 25 years, and they had two grown up children. On Sunday 5th December 2010 a Special Church Meeting had 75 members present, and the vote to invite Stephen to the pastorate was 73 in favour and 2 against. The invitation was readily accepted.

Completion on the sale of 5 Seaton Road took place on 17th December. There was decorating and some repair work to be carried out, and the family moved into the new manse in March 2011. The Induction Service, formally bringing the Pastoral Vacancy to an end, was held on Saturday 2nd April. Rev Mike Stanbrook led the service; Rev Paul Kerley, the Regional Minister, performed the act of induction. The preacher was Rev David Rogers who had trained for the ministry with Stephen at Regents Park College, Oxford, in the 1980s.

[1] 'Storming Home' was published in 2013 by Monarch Books

THE UNFINISHED STORY

Since 2011 the church has made several changes and received a number of encouragements. The car park belonging to the building on the corner of Canterbury Street was made available for the church to use at weekends, making life considerably easier for the congregation. A new sign was constructed for the front of the church building presenting a more prominent face to the public. The church toilets were also substantially redeveloped in 2012 at a cost of £15,000. This was made possible by some generous gifts as well as a donation in memory of Muriel Greenslade who passed away that year.

In 2012 the church began exploring how it could deal with the problem of personal debt which is a major social problem in Medway. Through meetings with Christians Against Poverty (CAP) the church agreed to open a CAP Debt Centre in June 2013. Ruth Millard has been employed part time to act as Centre Manager and Debt Coach. The initiative gained considerable support from the church, and has proved to be an enormous benefit to a number of families as well as an effective Christian outreach into the community.

Numbers attending on Sunday mornings began to grow and the balcony was re-opened in the summer of 2011. The Congregation Count submitted to the Baptist Union in 2011 reported an average Sunday morning attendance of 135 adults and children. In 2012 the equivalent figure was 147. The church membership figure, however, has not risen above 165. In the past three years the church carried out a revision of the membership roll with some twenty names being removed, and several more resignations. At the same time twenty five new members joined the church. The church also managed to reconnect with over a dozen members who had stopped attending during the latter part of the Pastoral Vacancy.

A Sunday afternoon service (from 5.30pm) was launched in the Lighthouse preceded by tea. This runs in three eight-week blocks in the spring, summer and autumn. It averages over thirty people, and has proved very popular with those unable to access the main church on a Sunday morning. A monthly Men's Breakfast was launched in one of the local pubs. And new forms of church have been experimented with including "Messy

Church", which proved very popular with some of the parents attending the Monday morning toddler group, Steps.

Staffing levels at Children's Church have increased allowing the church to provide a full age-related programme for children each Sunday. Week day activities have increased to such an extent that it has been very difficult to accommodate the number of user-groups wanting to access the premises. In partnership with St Mark's Church we have provided the base for a weekly gathering of international students called "Tabletalk" led by Lynne Martin. An arrangement with Medway Council also enables a series of cookery classes for adults with learning difficulties to take place.

Ministries started in earlier periods continued to be effective throughout this period. The Tuesday afternoon Prime Time provides a service of worship and fellowship for upwards of two dozen people, many of whom are unable to attend on Sunday mornings. Leadership of this group passed to Kath Greening and Joan Johnson once Hazel Mitchell had retired. When Brad and Kath Greening moved to Eastbourne in 2012, other people rose to the occasion to support Joan in heading up this valuable work.

The Wednesday morning coffee shop (or 'Friendship Morning' as it is now called) continues to provide a valuable service for a number of local residents. Led by Brenda and Alun Wintle it provides a 'thought for the day' each week which always seems to be appreciated by those who attend. The Craft Time continues to run fortnightly on a Thursday morning. Numbers attending have reached upwards of 90, and leadership of the group has been shared between Anne Newnham, Margaret Howlett, Daphne Abbott and Penny Wyatt. A monthly Friday Lunch Club has been run by the church catering manager, Liz Clark. With the support and encouragement of staff at Prime Time and the CAP Centre the numbers attending this have been creeping up towards fifty. Bill Clark continues to run the Word on the Street charity in the Vineries. In the last couple of years the work has expanded both in Gillingham and also in Gravesend where a similar project has started.

One of the biggest changes over this period took place in the life of the Brigades. In 2012 the Girls Brigade were experiencing a shortage of staff. This became critical once Jane Wood, the GB Captain, decided to step down. Changes to the national Boys Brigade Constitution allowed for the formation of a Girls Association as part of a BB Company, and consequently, in consultation with the girls and their parents, the Girls Brigade Company closed. In September 2012 a new-look Boys Brigade Company with Girls Association was launched. All the girls from the old Company came over and joined the new organisation. In 2013 Ken Davey retired as Boys Brigade Captain after 25 years. His place was taken by his son, Craig Davey.

Prayer remained central to the life of the church, and answers to prayer came in the form of two wonderful healing miracles. In 2012 Lyn Newlan became gravely ill following planned surgery. As elder and Treasurer, her role in the church was invaluable and her recovery was a cause of much rejoicing. At the same time Geoff Bowe was diagnosed with severe pancreatitis. After twelve months in Kings College Hospital, London, he finally returned home several stones lighter but glad to be alive.

Sadly the same period saw the home-call of a number of long standing church members. In 2011 Arthur Johnson passed away. He had been the church organist for many years, and brought a wealth of experience and talent to his role. Muriel Greenslade died the following year, and in 2013 Barbara Eames passed away soon after celebrating her 99th birthday. Barbara had been a school teacher, and a life-long friend of Israel. Kind, gracious, learned and beautifully spoken, Barbara's smile and twinkling eyes are sorely missed. Later that same year Val Brown and Derek Winn tragically passed away. In 2014 the church was deeply saddened by the sudden and unexpected death of Sandra Greening.

The summer of 2014 also saw the retirement of Fred Adams from his role as Church Adminstrator. Fred had carried out this role for 12 years and brought both a professionalism and spiritual maturity to the post. His presence in the Church office on Monday and Wednesday mornings will be greatly missed. Cheryl Keating takes his place as Administrator.

A new leadership team was formed in November 2013. Jim Beadle, Steve Carr, Joy David, Martin Green, Roy Jones and Adam Peake were elected as deacons to serve alongside Albert Barnes, Hilary Cox, Steve Powell and

Paul Wintle. Lyn Newlan and Stephen Greasley continue to serve as elders.

Perhaps the most problematic issue during this period was the age-old dilemma of what to do with the church buildings. Although they had been well maintained in the previous ten years, the old Victorian buildings were perceived to be hampering the mission of the church. There were steep steps to the front entrance of the worship area; an austere, confusing and unwelcoming frontage; a wholly inadequate, dated and inaccessible lift; and a shortage of toilet facilities at the first floor level. There were also visibility issues in large parts of the balcony ever since the floor level around the old pulpit area had been lowered some years earlier.

In 2012 some thought was given to whether the church should look to relocate to a different site within Gillingham – perhaps in partnership with another church - but this looked to be financially prohibitive. So, during 2013, further thought was given to refurbishing the front entrance area and the worship space itself. The church employed Canterbury-based architect Nick Lee-Evans who put together an ambitious design for reconfiguring the front entrance area. A guide price of £750,000 was attached to the scheme, and in 2014 decisions will need to be made as to whether to pursue this project or consider some other solution to the perceived problems. A 'Fund for the Future' was launched in January 2014, and a Gift Day and other fund raising strategies have helped the church towards its target.

On Sunday 27th April 2014 the church celebrated its 135th Church Anniversary. It has been a remarkable story. It is also an unfinished story. While the fundamental message the church proclaims remains the same – a message of Good News to a needy world and a needy people – the expression and demonstration of that Good News will continue to evolve. New ministries will emerge and new projects, all designed to flesh out God's love for the people of the town. What motivated those early pioneers back in the 1870s continues to inspire us still. A church of 160 members is only a third of the size it was in the 1920s and the 1980s. But with energy, drive and vision, and a fundamental belief in a remarkable God, Jesus' words in Matthew 17:20 remain our confidence and inspiration: "Nothing will be impossible for you."

Appendix 1

In 1985 the Leprosy Mission published a series of Meditations and Prayers by Eddie Askew. The collection was entitled 'Many voices, one voice.' One of those meditations was based on the author hearing Tom and Doreen Rogers testimony at the Baptist Assembly in 1984:

Mark 16:1-7

I HAVE just seen the resurrection — or something very like it. A married couple were interviewed at a meeting I attended. Two years ago Doreen was told she had serious cancer. After surgery, the cancer recurred. Last year she was told she'd probably die before Christmas. Her husband, Tom, is a Baptist minister. A year ago the diagnosis was made that he too needed surgery for cancer. They are both still under medical treatment.

It was an honest and moving interview. They'd not found it easy to come to terms with what had happened, with dying, or with not being around any more; or with the thought that one could be left, lonely. But they'd found *today*. Accept today, they said, use it, experience it to the full, enjoy it. Don't worry about the future, today is wonderful. "Spring, this year, has never been so beautiful," said Doreen.

Listening to them, watching them, I suddenly realised that you don't need to die to experience the resurrection. It was there in front of me. In the courage. Of course, they've "died". I guess that in facing the stark realities before them, they've died many deaths. Values and attitudes that seemed important must have changed, or disappeared. But Doreen and Tom were alive, are alive, with a quality of life I can't describe but which I can feel and identify.

Someone has described Christians as people of the resurrection living in a Good Friday world. Tom and Doreen certainly are. I don't know what the future holds for them, and neither do they. In one sense it's important, in another sense it doesn't matter at all, because they've begun to live in the resurrection. Hallelujah! Christ is risen.

Appendix 2

On 12th May 1989 the 'Chatham News' carried an article entitled 'Amazing Couple.' While ostensibly about Tom and Doreen Rogers it dealt particularly with their care of an elderly blind man called Sid Williams of Barnsole Road. Tom and Doreen had taken an interest in Sid and had provided a degree of support for him. As a result of this kindness Sid left the bulk of his £136,000 estate to the Tom and Doreen Rogers Memorial Fund. It was this legacy which was principally responsible for the Memorial Fund reaching such an impressive amount. And it was this legacy which was principally responsible for the dream of Rogers House becoming a reality.

Amazing couple

The Rev. Tom Rogers and his wife Doreen.

The Chatham News published details of a will. And from those few paragraphs, the story has unfolded of a remarkable Gillingham clergyman and his wife.

Tom Rogers was minister at Gillingham Baptist Church for more than 20 years and, with his wife Doreen, spread his own brand of kindness which will be remembered for years.

One person who certainly never forgot the friendship shown was Sid Williams, formerly of Barnsole Road. He left the bulk of his £136,000 estate to the Tom and Doreen Rogers Memorial Fund.

And the report of his will has brought a response from clerk to the trustees of the fund Mr. David King.

Mr. King has told of Tom and Doreen's work for the elderly and needy over many years.

Sid was taken under their wing when he was old and blind and was so grateful that he changed his will just before his death.

Tom and Doreen showed great bravery when they were both diagnosed as having cancer while in their early 50s.

They continued their work, often in great pain, but died in the autumn of 1987. The memorial fund is raising money to build an Abbeyfield extra-care home at Wigmore, named in their memory.

146

Appendix 3